Arthur Bunyan Caldwell

A Lecture of the History of Harlem

Arthur Bunyan Caldwell

A Lecture of the History of Harlem

ISBN/EAN: 9783337086497

Printed in Europe, USA, Canada, Australia, Japan

Cover: Foto ©ninafisch / pixelio.de

More available books at **www.hansebooks.com**

HISTORY OF HARLEM

----- BY----- -

A. B. Caldwell,

THE
HISTORY OF HARLEM

----- BY -----

COL. A. B. CALDWELL.

An Historical Narrative delivered at Harlem Music Hall, April 24th, 1882, before a very large and highly appreciative audience.

THE GREATEST SUCCESS OF FIFTY LECTURES.

It embraces a full and succinct history of two hundred and forty-three years, giving stirring events of the Revolution; the new settlement of Harlem; struggles with the Indians; description of old landmarks still standing; improvements of Harlem contrasted with the "new harlem," and many amusing anecdotes.

TOGETHER WITH APPENDIX OF HISTORY OF NEW YORK, FROM 1598 TO 1674.

ALSO A BUSINESS DIRECTORY OF HARLEM.

NEW YORK:
Small Talk Publishing Comp
1882.

PREFACE.

In presenting this book to our Patrons, and a generous Public, but little need be said. The Lecture emenating from the well known ability of Col. Caldwell, as a writer and public speaker, will commend itself to every lover of history; it being a complete narrative of Harlem, and told in an entertaining style. Of the entire lecture course of the Young Men's Hebrew Association of Harlem, of about fifty in number, delivered in Music Hall last winter by prominent speakes the lecture of Col. Caldwell drew forth the largest and most intelligent audience, was the finest delivered, and received the greatest plaudits. It was a complete and triumphant success in the lecture field, and was followed by an imperative demand for the publication of the lecture. Col. Caldwell gave us, free of charge, his manuscript, to whom we offer our public thanks.

This History details the discovery of Harlem, the early pioneer's struggles with the Indians; formation of "New Harlem Village" and its government ; stirring incidents of the Revolution—one of the greatest battles thereof; old land-marks of the village and the Revolution now standing ; humorous and amusing anecdotes ; progress of tradesmen and mechanics; the good results which will arise from the Harlem River Improvement, and much other valuable information as to dates and historical incidents not heretofore published. Embracing a period of incidents since 1639 to date— 243 years (137 years prior to the Revolution.)

Also an interesting appended history of New York, from 1598 to 1674.

Also a Business Directory of the leading business firms in Harlem, all of which will be valuable information to every inhabitant of Manhattan Island.

PERKINSON & JOHNSON,

Publishers.

Harlem, July, 1882.

NOTICES OF THE PRESS.

[From the District Court Record]

On being introduced by President Carvalho, of the Y. M. H. A. of Harlem, the Colonel was received with immense applause, and entered immediately upon his work, in a loud and distinct voice, which he held for one hour and a half, enchaining the large and intelligent audience by thrilling incidents of the Revolution in Harlem; how the white settlers struggled with the aborigines 137 years prior to the Revolution, and giving a list of the progenitors of the present most prominent descendants of Harlem and their characteristics. * * * * The Colonel was at times truly eloquent, arousing his hearers to the highest pitch of enthusiasm; and it is evident that he will soon become a very popular lecturer, taking this demonstration among his numerous friends, and where he is well known as a writer and public speaker.

[From the N. Y. Star.]

Music Hall, Harlem, was filled last night with a fine audience, to hear a lecture by Colonel A. B. Caldwell on "Harlem, its History and Prosperity." Many of the descendants of the early settlers were present, and old Dutch names abounded, both in the lecture and in the house.

[From the Harlem Record.]

A lecture was delivered on Monday evening at Harlem Music Hall by Col. A. B. Caldwell on "Harlem as It Was, as It Is, and as It Will Be." There was a goodly attendance of people, many of them being the representatives of the old Harlem families. The lecture was a good effort, reflecting credit on the patient research and industry of the lecturer.

[From the Westchester Times]

A very interesting lecture on the History of Harlem was delivered Monday evening, at Harlem Music Hall, under the auspices of the Young Men's Hebrew Association of Harlem, by Colonel Alonzo B. Caldwell. The hall was crowded with an attentive audience, a great many of whom, no doubt, were descendants of the early settlers. The lecture is entirely original with Col. Caldwell, and that gentleman deserves great credit for the pains he has bestowed on the subject, for, besides searching through old documents, letters, etc., he has thoroughly canvassed the whole district whose history he gives and brought many historical facts to light. The Colonel spoke in a loud, voice, distinctly audible in every part of the hall, and applause was frequent. He introduced many humorous stories, which he told in a funny manner, and his discourse was thus relieved of the tedium generally experienced at an historical lecture and the audience was kept in good humor.

[From the N. Y. Independent.]

The Colonel held the attention of his hearers during the hour and a half occupied, and was frequently interrupted by long continued and hearty applause. He showed a keen appreciation of his subject, and handled the same with a masterly skill,

[From the N. Y. Tribune.]

Colonel A. B. Caldwell lectured last night at the Harlem Music Hall, Third Avenue and 130th Street, on the early settlement of Harlem village. He detailed incidents concerning its government, its early inhabitants, and its old historic landmarks, many of which are now standing. He closed with the prediction that the Harlem River improvements now going on will make Harlem the most important centre of the metropolis. A large audience was present.

LECTURE ON HARLEM.

Mr. President, Ladies and Gentlemen:—

By the kindness and courtesy of the popular Young Men's Hebrew Association of Harlem, I have the honor to stand before you this evening to deliver an essay, but with no little embarrassment, as they have given me a theme for discourse more suited for older residents of Harlem and abler speakers who are here to-night, and could give their subject more embellishments, and render its annals more attractive and entertaining.

However, as a citizen of this historic soil, I will make my best endeavors not to weary your patience, nor recount facts which are not fully authenticated by truthful history. To my subject then, " Harlem, Its Past History; Its Present and Future Prosperity." It would be a long story to trace the ancestry of the Harlem pioneers: it would carry us back to the fatherlands, to the great marts and to some of the obscure homes of Holland, Belgium, and Northern France—amid their antique remains and rare works of art, the standard wonders of tourists from every clime in the world. The astounding discoveries of Columbus in the fifteenth century had opened up a new field for maritime adventure in this then vast wilderness of ours. It was the heroic enterprise of the merchants and mariners of the French seaports under Louis XII., which first thoroughly explored the North American coast and discovered that exhaustless mine of wealth in the Newfoundland fisheries of the New World.

The idea of colonizing America, slumbered in France during its civil wars, and was revived in the time of Henry the Fourth. Hence Champlain in 1608, founded Quebec, the first permanent European colony in North America.

Holland now appears on the scene as a rival adventurer and explorer, having enriched herself in the East India trade. Hudson an Englishman, who had discovered the famous river which still bears his name, sold his rights of discoveries here to the Hollanders when her merchants and capitalists fitted him out at Amsterdam in 1609, and he made further explorations up the river, and led to the formation of the celebrated "Dutch West India Company;" and in 1623, the first colonists, consisting of French and Walloons, who were driven by war and persecution, took refuge on the banks o the Hudson River. From this small beginning grew the great stat New York, the "Empire of the Union."

Before I come to the Harlem settlement, please indulge me in a brief retrospective review. It is an old error cherished in thi locality that the founders of Harlem all came from Holland They came from several parts of Western Europe—from the sunny plains of France, and from the fir-clad hills of Scandinavia. Danes Swedes and Norwegians, in faith Lutherans—men of integrity, and used to toil and hardships. The large proportion, however, were Hollanders and French Huguenots. Ams. '.. was the great commercial mart of Holland, the point of immigration to the "New Netherlands," which tract of land then called, covered New England through to Virginia, including New York city, the "New Amsterdam."

Your time and patience would not allow me to picture the cause which led all of our New York or Harlem pioneers to seek thi land—to sunder the national ties of their respective Fatherlands after many struggles for civil and religious liberty, and to escape vasselage. This you can find in history. I am limited to local facts—to deal with Harlem as it was, is, and what it is to become. Although this is an historical essay, I must leave the dry, heavy annals to the historian. The objects of history are not merely the recording of facts. The world,—as its distant and widely extending climes, with their peculiarities of situation and climate, make together one great whole,—so that the events that have happened in it, which are happening, and which will happen, are closely interwoven, as it were, into one unbroken thread. The past has had its influence in forming the present. The present is operating mightily on the future. History may, yes, it must note down events, when and where they occur. It must inform us of Cæsar, of Leonidas, of Bonepart, Cromwell and Washington, and other great men,—when they lived, what distinguished actions they achieved, what land they blessed or ruined,—how they rose, and how they fell. It must also take notice of the smaller characters, who take part in the great drama of Life. And how beautiful, how grand, how ennobling is this view of mankind and their doings. Ages have rolled on—generation has succeeded generation, but the tie that connects man with his fellow man, has never been severed. They, who have gone before, by their gradual advancement, have contributed to place us where we are ; and we, in our turn, are but carrying on the same great enterprise of improvement, in which they have labored. There is not a great event in the annals of the world, wherever or by whom achieved, that has ceased to operate, or that ever will. There is not a distinguished character,—be it for his virtues, or his crimes,—who has ever trod upon the earth, who does not yet live in the good or ill influence of his life. Is it not a pleasant thought, that men of all ages, and all nations, are thus fellow laborers, are thus brethren? Is it not a high and interesting duty, which, in this view, history has in charge?

The present is a revolutionary age. The political elements seem everywhere in motion,—and all are busy, either as actors in, or spectators of, the great work, as it is called, of reform. And while new revolutions are in progress, old ones are becoming the themes of conversation, and the subjects of research. Men are going back to the ancient battlefields of their fellow men,—studying the principles which gave birth to their uprisings, noting the connections of remarkable events, and writing the lives of the leaders of revolutions. All this is natural, it is well, it is just, it is right.

But to resume. The opportunities for traffic in furs on the Hudson, the flattering advantages for peaceable homes and lovely landscapes, and an acquisition for riches, had long attracted Holland and other countries to emigrate to " New Amsterdam," or the Island of New York, or what the Indians called it, *Manahatta*, signifying the " Red Men's Home." Our early settlers here were not criminals, escaping from justice, nor speculators allured by plunder, nor vagabonds exiled from their native lands, but they were honest, intelligent, hard-working and useful citizens, whose love for civil and religious liberty, and their devotion to their religious tenets were further incentives which induced them to leave tyranny and seek what has ever since been called the "Asylum of the Oppressed," or, in a more poetic sense,

"The land of the free and the home of the brave."

I will omit the details of Hudson's explorations of Long Island, New York and the Hudson River; that on the spot now called the "Battery," the "Fort Amsterdam" was then built to protect the traders in 1614; that up to 1656, New York contained only 120 houses and 1,000 inhabitants; how the Dutch surrendered to the English, and afterwards recaptured their beloved city, and soon afterwards ceded it to the English by treaty, on conclusion of the war between Holland and England; nor the frequent conflicts between the Indians and the white men of those days; how the tea was served out (as was said) of "majestic delft teapots, ornamented with pictures of fat little Dutch shepherds and shepherdesses tending pigs; how the beaux distinguished themselves by their adroitness in replenishing this pot from a huge copper tea-kettle, which would have made the pigmy macaronies of these degenerate days perspire merely to look at. To sweeten the beverage, a lump of sugar was laid beside each cup, and the company alternately nibbled and sipped with great decorum, until a shrewd and economic Dutch vrow invented an improvement, which was to suspend a large lump of sugar directly over the tea table, by a string from the ceiling, so that it could be swung from mouth to mouth. There was no flirting or coquetting in those days—no gambolling of old ladies, nor hoyden chattering and romping of young ones—nor self-satisfied struttings of wealthy gentlemen," with more cents in their pockets than sense in their heads, nor amusing conceits and monkey divertisements of smart young gentlemen, with no brains at all. No fast horses and defalcations in banks, nor swindled treasuries. Then the young men earned the dollars and the fathers saved them; but now the fathers earn the fortunes and their sons and daughters spend them! On the contrary, the young ladies of our early days "seated themselves demurely in their rush-bottomed chairs and knit their woolen hose, nor scarcely opened their mouths excepting to eat, and to say, ' Yah, mynher,' to every question asked of them ; behaving in all things like decent, well educated damsels, in true Holland style. As to the gentlemen, each of them tranquilly smoked his pipe and seemed lost in contemplation of the blue and white tiles with which the fireplaces were decorated ; wherein sundry passages of Scripture were portrayed. Tobit and his dog figured to great advantage ; Haman swung conspicuously and nervously on his gibbet, and Jonah appeared most mournfully bouncing out of the whale like harlequin through a barrel of fire!

The fair damsels' hair, models of untortured abominations of modern art, was scrupulously pomatumed back from their foreheads with candle-grease, covered with little caps of quilted calico, which fitted exactly to their heads." Those were good old honest days, when Mary Ann gossipers were unknown, every woman staid at home and read her Bible, tended her own babies, scorned all lap dogs, and wore large side pockets to carry about ordinary household utensils, such as big shears, pot hooks, wooden ladles, iron spoons and clay snuff-boxes.

We now leave the " down town " of Manhattan and go to the " East end" as the Harlem bergers termed it then. The Indians had full mastery of the forest hereabout. Their hickory bows were six feet long, and when pulled on man or beast, few escaped the deadly arrow. They lived by fishing and hunting, and clothed their bodies with the skins of animals, and covered their huts with the barks of trees. They used flint or stone hatchets, and stone pipes for smoking tobacco. There were two races, the Manettoes, on this side of Harlem River, and, on the other side, in Westchester county, the Wickquaskeeks. When the white man's axe commenced to fell trees on the Island, and thatched houses were being built, these dusky creatures, as they passed to and fro on their trading expeditions, eyed with surprise and displeasure the incursions and inroads made upon their ancient hunting grounds by the " pale faces." The howl of the wolf, the plaintive scream of the panther and the shrill yell of the redman, often disturbed the deathlike stillness of night, striking terror to the hearts of the suddenly awakened sleepers of this locality.

Although Wm. Kieft was Governor of the " New Netherlands,"

which included all of this part of the country, the Indians disputed his right either to the land or their government here, and acknowledged no ruler except "Manitto," an imaginary "Great Spirit," from whom they traditionally believed they had emanated, and, as aborigines, they possessed this soil, and declared : "White man no good; Indian drive off pale faces." This savage hatred was soon manifested against our first settlers, as I shall fully show. Captain Jochiem Pictersen Kuyter, of Holstein, who had formerly commanded in the East Indies, for the King of Denmark, with his friend Jonas Bronck, and their respective families, came here by way of Amsterdam, in 1639. Kuyter was a brave, adventurous man, finely educated, and possessed of considerable means. He brought with him laborers and a good breed of cattle. To find immediate grazing for his stock, he obtained a grant of land from Governor Kieft, called by the Indians, "Schorakin," lying along the Harlem River, comprising about 400 acres. He built a thatched-roof dwelling and out-buildings, enclosed all with a high palisade fence, as protection against the savages and wild beasts. He called his Bowerie or Plantation, *Zegendal*, or "Vale of Blessing," or in other words, "Happy Valley." This land lay in the vicinity between East 107 to 113th Streets, and from Harlem River to 3rd Avenue. Kuyter and his white followers had terrible struggles with the Indians. The red men were as savage as their cousins, the wolves and bears, and when this bestial trio fought for the products of the forest, the white men looked on as complacently and as indifferently as the Hoosier did when his wife fought the "bar," he "didn't care a darn which whipped "

The Indians, in 1653, burned Kuyter's house during the absence of himself and family. He soon built up again and went on bravely, keeping a watchful eye upon the Indians and tilling his plantation, and bringing it into a high state of cultivation, By his winning manners, and obliging the Indians on individual occasions, he had dispelled much of their personal animosity towards him, when Governor Kieft, by a most impolitic act, fired the entire Indian race with indignation ; by levying upon them a tax, and demanding their corn, fur and *Sewant*, (or *wampum*) in payment. This sewant was Indian money, made by tabular beads of pieces of conch shells, and fastened on skins, cloth or canvas. For many

years our early settlers used this sort of money in commercial
transactions, and even for church contributions. Only think, of
to-day, Colonel Samuel Waldron, who now sits on this platform, a
lineal descendant of the great Baron Resolved Waldron, (an early
pioneer of Harlem) sticking beaded canvas, on Sunday, into the contribution box of "Jimmy Wood's church."

The Indians grew more and more restive and troublesome as
their taxes were enforced. The white men had to carry arms, as
the red men were constantly in ambush, and had sworn " to root
out the Dutch." They ruthlessly killed off several white settlers
and burned their cabins, and believing that Kuyter could have
influenced a decrease in their taxes, or had a hand in the imposition, they resolved to murder him. The Weeksquakeck (Weschester)
Indians, came over stealthily in canoes, at midnight, in 1654, and
shot blazing arrows into his thatched roof, and as he came out in
front of his burning dwelling and bravely faced the savage enemies,
they pierced him to the heart with arrows, and he fell dead, which
was a mournful loss to the white settlers. His wife and children,
by going out the back way, escaped in the forest, and thus saved
their lives.

Other settlers of prominence had arrived in Harlem, almost co-
temporaneous with Kuyter, such as Isaac De Forrest, Dr. Johannes De La Montagne, Jonkheer Van Curler, etc. Isaac was the
ancestor of all the De Forrests hereabout. He settled on the
" Flats," was a tobacconist, a brewer, became a member of the
" Board of Selectmen," held several other public offices, and died
in 1674. Van Curler came over with Van Twiller (subsequently a
Director General,) possessed the " Otter spoor," situated north of
" Mill Creek," at 108th Street, and extending from Harlem River
to 5th Avenue. It lay next to De Forest's plantation. Dr.
Montagne was a French Hugenot, and it is safe to say that he
was the most learned scientist on Manhattan Island, and his ability
was courted by the highest in power. Governor Kieft appointed
him commander of a battallion of soldiers which the Doctor raised
himself, and he set out in pursuit of the Indians. He fought the
dusky races from Long Island to Harlem, and drove the affrightened
wretches to White Plains, there slaughtered many, burned their
main villages, and hostilities ceased for a long time, except by an

occasional marauding party. For this heroic service the Governor gave him a tract of land on the " Flats," lying between what is now called 94th and 108th streets, and from East River to 8th Avenue. He called his Bowerie " *Vredendal*," or " *Quiet Vale*," nearly a mile below the " New Harlem " village. The Doctor sold it to John L. Bogart for 3,000 guilders, ($750) in 1672 ; it was purchased in 1706 by Johannes Benson, the first Benson settler here ; and the property was held by the Benson family, until Margaret Benson, sole surviving owner married Andrew McGown, in 1784. Portions of this tract are still owned by the McGown family. The well-known Thompson family, (George Thompson corner 3d Avenue and 125th street) are descendants of Dr. Montagne. The Doctor raised eight children here, the most prominent of whom was John Montagne. One of the descendants owned a piece of land, now within Central Park, upon which stood the Black Horse Tavern, of Revolutionary notoriety. Hon. Isaac Montagne, editor of the *Independent*, at Goshen, N. Y., is a lineal descendant of the Doctor. I have a quit-claim deed, given by twelve persons to James A. Corse, dated December, 1847, and among the signers are John De La Montagne, Geo. S. De La Montagne, Benjamin Thompson, (said George's father) John S. and Andrew Thompson, (uncles to George) and Eliza Thompson (George's aunt), which relinquishes all their interests in the Montagne property, called by the Indians, " *Rechewanes*," and deeded to the Doctor by Governor Kieft in 1647, as before stated. This is due proof that the Thompson family and the Montagne family are connexions by consanguinity.

Adjoining the Montagne farm was Baron Resolved Waldron's grant, lying between 81st and 94th Streets, and from Harlem River to 6th Avenue. The Indians called the Waldron Tract, also, *Rechewanes*, (crooked land) and by the Hollanders it was named "Hoorn's Hook," from an amusing incident. It appears that a surveyor named Jan Van Hoorn was with a surveying party in the forest there, and he volunteered one day to climb a tree for wild grapes. After filling his stomach and pockets with the coveted fruit, he proceeded to descend, fell, and the seat of his buckskin trowsers caught on a limb, and there he hung and swung, like a scare-crow in a cornfield, or like Mohammed's coffin, between the heavens and earth. The Hollanders beneath the tree observing the swivel predicament Hoorn was in, laughingly cried out, "See, Hoorn is hooked," and hence the appellation "Horns Hook," which lasted over 150 years among the Harlem settlers.

In this connection I might allude to the fact that Ex-Governor Kieft set sail for Holland, 1647, in the ship "Princess," which foundered, and was lost on the coast of Wales. General Petrus Stuyvesant had succeeded him as Governor, and appointed Baron Resolved Waldron, Joseph Waldron, (his brother) and Joost Van O. Blinus, as Commissioners to settle the "East End,"—Harlem. It was conditioned that they should plant twenty-five families here in three years, and establish a ferry across the river to Westchester, and call this side "New Harlem," which conditions were duly complied with. A row-boat with two oars conveyed foot passengers and horses, while mules and cattle had to swim behind the boat. This ferry was located on this side of 125th Street, east of First Avenue, then called "foot of the Church Lane." Soon was built there, what was since termed, "The Old Stone Ferry House," kept by Jan Van Riper, a jolly Holland Dutchman, who is thus described by one of Harlem's pastoral Bards :—

> "Who sold cider, bier and gin,
> Also kept good cheer within ;
> And for years his old sign hung,
> Most merrily by the breezes swung."

From the fact that so many weddings were had in this ancient mansion, it was called by the down-town people the "Wedding House." Many an elopement terminated in a wedding there, while some were intercepted and frustrated. The fastest horses won the day on that score. Van Riper, through a little cunning, used to help the young folks out. He would dose the "old man" with "stone fence," until he became jolly, then obtain his consent to the marriage, marry the happy young couple, when all, dominie included, indulged in "stone fence," and the connubial parties would merrily go home together. This old land-mark was last occupied by John Moore, and pulled down about twenty-one years ago.

Immigration to this country was now in full blast. Those who came over here the earliest, returned for visits, and each one gave glowing accounts of the richness of this country; its fine mineral, agricultural and commercial advantages, and particularly the personal liberties, or freedom from monarchial restraints, which the people enjoyed in the "New Netherlands," and especially on Manhattan Island. I might mention one of these return voyages as important. During the life time of Kuyter, he and Cornelius Melyn quarrelled with Governor Kieft, alleging that they had suffered losses through Kieft's misrule, while Governor; they being both members of the "Eight Men," or Council, wrote home to the States General, in the name of their Board, severe criticisms on Kieft's maladministration, which no doubt led to Kieft being superseded by Governor Stuyvesant. Kieft preferred charges against Kuyter and Melyn, and July 25th, 1647, both were tried, convicted and sentenced to be banished three years, and fined several hundred guilders. Stuyvesant, in passing sentence, quoted only the scriptural law for their offences--"*Thou shalt not speak evil of the ruler of thy people.*" Kieft was jubilant over his victory. Having amassed a fortune, he started on a visit to Holland, August 16th, 1647, in the ship "Princess," as I mentioned before, and curiously, the two banished culprits were put on board this same ship. The ship got out of its course, off the coast of Wales, struck a rock and began to sink. Kieft seeing all hope gone, acknowledged to Kuyter and Melyn that he did them wrong, and asked and obtained their forgiveness. The ship dashed to pieces, but Kuyter and Melyn were saved on seperate pieces of the wreck by drifting ashore, while Kieft and others met a watery grave, or more poetically speaking :

"In the deep blue ocean buried."

Melyn lost a son in this disaster, and also was engulphed Everardus Bogardus, the pastor, counselor and friend of Kuyter, Dr. Montagne, DeForests, Bronck and other colonists, whose death was long and deeply mourned by them. Kuyter and Melyn, after recovering from their shock, proceeded to Holland, laid their cases before the Prince of Orange, and bore back to Governor Stuyvesant a nullification of the order of banishment and fines. Kuyter remained the firm friend of his fellow compatriot Melyn, until his own tragic death, by the Indians, in 1654, as previously described. This furnishes the believers in fore-ordination an incident, "that a man born to be hung will never be drowned."

We now come to the year 1658, when a movement for a village was made. The incentive was on account of the insolvency of nearly all the land-holders hereabout. Most of the old farm owners had died, and their heirs had bankrupted the estates. Even Dr. Montague, who came here soon after Kuyter, had deeply involved his fine farm on the flats, and though a Vice Director General, with a recently increased salary, he was reduced to penury and want. The Kuyter heirs were no better off—in fact, there was a general depression all round, and everybody was in financial distress. It was resolved to form a village corporation, lay out and sell lots, and thus raise a sufficiency of money to retrieve their waning fortunes. Consequently the Director General and Council of "New Amsterdam" granted a village charter on March 4th, 1658, which embraced the Kuyter estate, the Conrad Van Keulen tract (200 acres) called then "Van Keulen's Hook, or originally named "Otter-Spoor," lying in the vicinity of 108th Street; also the Claes C. Swits' farm, which lay between the other two plantations, upon which latter farm the cleared portion was to form the village site. Ground was broken for it August 14th, and the survey was completed by September 10th, that year, when Johan Verveelen regaled a large company of the pioneer Bergers in festivity, with his "New Amsterdam Beer," amid great hilarity and good cheer which marked the auspicious event. The original plan of "New Harlem" village run from 74th Street, East River, diagonally to 128th Street, intersecting the Hudson or North River, taking inside all land lying between the Hudson and Harlem Rivers up to *Spuyten Duyvel* Creek. Many have asked why this creek was thus called. Well, I have three versions—take your choice. One is that Anthony Van Corlaer, the jolly trumpeter of Governor Stuyvesant, swore he would swim that stream on a dark, stormy night, in *spuyt den duyvel*, (in spite of the devil) and he was not as fortunate as Leander who swam the Hellespont, as his Satanic majesty, in the form of a mossbunker, seized Anthony and took

him "down below," to that warm place where they don't bank the
fire o'nights! Another tradition is, that the Indians called it after
Hudson's ship as it sailed up the creek, like a spouting devil, in
Dutch language, *Spuyten Duyvel*. Still another is given, in ancient
record, 1672, called *spuyten duyvel*, owing to a large spring flow-
ing into the creek. That creek is there still, but the "*duyvel* only
knows" where the name came from.

But to the village again. It was laid out along the "Great
Kill" (Harlem River), taking for its principle street an Indian
trail, touching the river at about 125th Street, where the Ferry
which I have described, passed over to "Broncksider," (Morrisania).
Another street was formed, called the "Great Way," but since that
time, has been better known as "Church Lane," with its historic
old homes and majestic elms--all gone to decay. Between these
two large streets, lay the erven, or house plots, ninety-three English feet long, and nearly as wide, while the cross streets formed
these into four lots each. That "Old Church Lane" still lives in
the fondest memories of our oldest inhabitants. They remember
the old Dutch Church, which stood near Harlem River, in a corner
of the cemetery removed in 1868.

The new village was laid out after the Holland style, into house
lots and garden plots adjoining, as desired for horticulture. It
will be observed that "New Amsterdam," (New York), and "New
Harlem" (our Harlem), and the ancient Amsterdam and Harlem,
in Holland, bear a dual resemblance, on account of the two cities
on either side of the ocean being near to the other, and possessing
similar advantages and relations. The Hollanders held their Harlem in great reverence—a synonym for all that was virtuous and
truly heroic, as the name is derived from two words, Heer and
Lem, Lord Willem being the founder of Harlem, in Holland.

At the formation of New Harlem village, a violent malarial dis-
temper broke out, and many persons died of the disease. Besides,
floods came and despoiled fruits, crops and winter forage, and
nearly created a famine. Many occupants abandoned their plots,
but new settlers took them up in the spring, and business moved
right along, until 1669, when a war broke out between the white
settlers and Indians at Esopus, and a general massacre was feared,
on Manhattan Island, as emanating from the River Indians here,

who were in sympathy with the Mohicans at Esopus. This fact frightened many whites away from "New Amsterdam," as also from "New Harlem." Governor Stuyvesant took the field at Esopus, and determined to exterminate the hostile savages there, and gave orders to open on the Indians here, if they did not keep quiet. Our new village flew to arms, and every old blunderbus, shot gun, musket, horse pistol, sabre, and rusty sword were polished up, and put in position for the impending attack. In the absence of the Governor, the Council acted, and appointed a Board of Military Commissioners here, consisting of Jan Pieterson Slot, Daniel Tourneur and Jaques Creson, the first one named to be President. The villagers were put under this control, or Martial Law, and this was the first local authority exercised in "New Harlem." The Esopus war lasted about six months, during which time Harlem was kept in great disquietude.

Human nature seems to have been the same in Harlem, 222 years ago, as it is now, for we then found a mixed society—fights over cattle, swine and geese, breaking into enclosures ; and occasional street broils superinduced by too frequent potations of "New Amsterdam Beer," the slanderous tongue of an occasional Mary Ann setting gossip-mongers by the ears ; quarrels over disturbed landmarks, etc., all of which induced the better portion of the villagers to petition the Director General and Council for a "Court of Justice," which was granted August 16th, 1660, and Jan Pieterson Slot, Daniel Tourneur and Piere Creson, were appointed a Board of Magistrates, the first one named to act as *Schout*, (Deputy Sheriff.) The trials had before this board were numerous, and many very amusing. Having secured a Court, the people now turned their attention to church fellowship. They united into an organization, of the "Dutch Reformed" persuasion, with Jan La Montagne Jr., as Deacon. A young minister, Rev. Michael Zyperus, who arrived from Holland, October 25th, 1660, was selected as Pastor, but not having been ordained, he was allowed only to exhort, while the administration of sacrament, performances of baptism and marriages, and admissions to memberships, were left to Rev. Henry Selyns, of Brooklyn, who officiated in the chapel, on the site of the present St. Mark's Church, Stuyvesant Place,

New York. Zyperus held religious worship in the private houses, and other buildings in Harlem, no church being yet erected.

Daniel Tourneur, the ancestor of the Tourners, was appointed Magistrate for Harlem, August 16th, 1660, and he served various terms in that capacity, as also Deputy Sheriff several years, became a deacon in the church, and was selected a delegate to the General Assembly, in 1664.

In 1661, Adolpie Meyer arrived here. He was ancestor of the Meyers, and married Maria, daughter of Johanas Verveelen.

Arent Harmans Bussing several times Magistrate in Harlem, and ancestor of the Bussings here and in Westchester County, arrived here in 1661. One of the decendants, Rebecca D., married Hon. Nathaniel Jervis of New York, once known as Alderman and County Clerk. He is still living.

Jan Dyckman, one of the wealthiest patenters of Kingsbridge, came over here with Adolph Meyer and Arent H. Bussing, in 1661. He was the ancestor of all the Dyckmans hereabout.

At this time, 221 years ago, there being no grist mill here, the Harlemites carried their grists to Dutch Kills, Queens County. They conveyed them in canoes, through the dangers of Hell-gate to Newtown Creek, now 34th Street, and up that creek to Peter Joris' grist mill. This mill was taken down about fifty years ago, and the upper and nether mill stones are now embedded as door steps, in front of a residence 108 years old, within a few rods of the mill site. That mill was not a very lively one, as it ground out only three schepels per day (2 1-4 bushel). This year (1661) a petition was denied the Harlemites for a grist mill on Dr. Montagne's flat, for the reason that a new mill might form a settlement about it, and deter the progress of the "New Harlem" village.

The Hopper family is very numerous in New Jersey, Harlem and Westchester County. Andries Hopper the ancestor came here, from Holland, in 1652, and Yellis Hopper of "Hoorn's Hook," was grandfather to Mrs. William H. Colwell, now residing corner 125th Street and Lexington Avenue, Harlem; and to Mrs. Eliza Liscomb, who died and was buried in Woodlawn Cemetery in 1880. Mrs. Liscomb was a sister to Mrs. Colwell, and the mother of William H. Liscomb, Alfred A. Liscomb of Harlem, and Eliza J., wife of Archibauld G. Armour, in Westchester County.

The Delamater family sprung from Claude Le Maistre, who came here in 1662, and served as Magistrate four terms. Hon. Schuyler Colfax is one of his descendants.

The well-known Johannes Vermylea was the projenitor of the Vermylea family. He came here in 1662. He was captain of a military company in 1663, a court messenger in 1665, constable in 1667, magistrate two terms from 1670, and member of the committee of safety in 1689, and a brewer withal. He resided nearly central of block, between 1st and 2d Avenues and 122d and 123d Streets, and died in 1696.

Jan Louwe Bogert, ancestor of the Bogerts, came here in 1662. He was magistrate in 1675-6. He spent thirty-five years in Harlem and moved down town. One of his decendents bought the Lawrence Benson Homestead, and during the Revolution, when the Provincial Convention on leaving New York, met for a month in the Harlem Church, the records were kept at the Bogart Mansion, which stood then on the site of the present Morris Randell House, foot of 125th Street and Harlem River.

As immigrants were constantly arriving, the Montagues petitioned the Director General and Council to allow them new allotments of their tract Fredendal, but it was denied, in fear that a rival settlement might retard the growth of "New Harlem." Up to this date (1662) Harlem contained thirty-two heads of families, and of these Jan La Montagne Sr., had been the longest in this section, about twenty-five years, and Jan Laurens Duyts, the only one of the thirty-two who had been born here. Of this number eleven were French, four Walloons, a larger species of the French, seven Hollanders, four Danes, three Swedes and three Germans. A braver or more honest lot of pioneers never graced a new country with their presence.

> " Oft did the harvest to their sickle yield,
>   Their furrow oft the stubborn glebe has broke;
> How jocund did they drive their team afield,
>   How bowed the woods beneath their sturdy stroke !
> Let not ambition mock their useful toil,
>   Their homely joys and destiny obscure ;
> Nor grandeur hear with a disdainful smile,
>   The short and simple annals of the poor."

The spirit which animated their breasts is rooted in the soft rich soil of Harlem, and although many of their decendants have been scattered over the inhabitable globe, that sweet memory of their once native Harlem, like the scent of the roses with the broken vase, will cling round them still!

That the surrounding lands should not go to waste, the Director General and Council finally ordered a new allotment of all the lands about the village, when ground briefs were discarded, and Van Keulen's Hook and the Montagne flat were divided up into twenty-two lots for new purchasers and leases. This enabled William Montagne to hold the "Montagne's Point" free of debt. At this time (1663) the old custom of "horning" newly married couples was in vogue. Soon as the marriage ceremony was over then commenced in front of the house the blowing of horns, firing of guns, blunderbuses, old Holland horse pistols, drumming of tin pans—such din only as Bedlam could let loose. After every tooter was tired of blowing, the party would plant "May Trees" in front of the nuptial door, filled with ragged stockings, etc. It was not infrequent that sometimes the window would suddenly rise and the horners get their eyes full of ground red pepper, and occasionally receive a volley of peas or beans fired out of an old shot gun. Several lives were lost on such occasions, as old crusty bachelor bridegrooms would not stand much of such clownish onsense.

June 7th, 1663, filled Harlem with alarm—the Indian massacre at Esopus. Our settlers then numbering in all forty adults, enclosed the village with a line of stockades, and everybody was armed, three seven pound ball cannon were planted, and the whole village became a garrisoned outpost. They broke up this valliant army of forty into four companies, and put a brave commander at each head, all resolving to give the Indians "fits," or be a good fit for the savages when they came on, as they expected the Indians hereabout to take sides with the race at Esopus. Stuyvesant, who seemed to need troops at Esopus, gave orders for aid, and our army here sent *eight* reinforcements, which came very near breaking up one of our companies! But it had a good effect abroad, as the Esopus Indians hauled off when they found out that the Hartein troops were on the march! Like Col. Crockett's Coon, "no shoot, Indian come down!"

The first land case which was tried in Harlem, January 16th, 1662, was between Nicholas De Meyer, Plaintiff, and Sigismundus Lucas, defendant. "Sig" sold his lot and refused to give possession, and of course, was defeated on his breach of contract.

The first town clerk elected in Harlem was John L. Montagne, the oldest son of the old Doctor, in 1662. John Verveelen came here January 13th, 1663, became a magistrate (*Schepen* in Dutch) in 1663, a delegate to the General Assembly in 1664, and died about 1702. He was associated in the brewing business with Isaac DeForest.

Baron Resolved Waldron, the ancestor of the Waldrons, came to this country with his brother Joseph, in 1654, and moved to Harlem in October, 1664. He was a printer in Germany. He held *Fiscael* (Attorney General) and various commissions and other offices of public trust. Col. Samuel Waldron, who resides on the corner of 113th Street and 4th Avenue, is one of his honored descendants, to whom I am deeply indebted for many valuable facts in this essay. And right here let me acknowledge much data obtained from Riker's History of Harlem.

In 1664, laborers were very scarce in Harlem, consequently on May 29th, that year, our settlers proceeded to Fort Amsterdam and purchased negroes at auction. They came from Curacao, in the ship Shannon. Hence, slavery was planted in "New Harlem." A new saw mill was erected this year by Jan Van Bommel, on a stream emptying into the East River, foot of 74th Street, since called "Saw Kill."

While Harlem was now prospering, the rest of the "New Netherlands" was in turmoil by one cause or another. The Dutch possessions were seized on the Connecticut River; a revolt broke out on Long Island and in Westchester, in alliance with New England, besides Indian troubles, all of which filled Stuyvesant with alarm. He finally allowed a General Assembly to meet at "New Amsterdam," April 10th, 1664, of the people's own chosen representatives, with Daniel Tourneur and Johannes Verveelen as the Harlem delegation. The convention had no authority to do anything, beyond an appeal to the States General in Holland, to aid in the defense of this section. May 18th, same year, concluded a treaty, which was ratified by the Hudson Indians and by those savages in and about Harlem. The Indian Chief Sanwenarack, of the Wickquaskecks of Westchester, having also signed the treaty, gave great security and encouragement to Harlem.

Soon came another alarm, one unlooked for. Col. Richard Nicolls, with an English fleet, suddenly appeared in the harbor; and September 16, 1664, Fort Amsterdam surrendered. Nicolls announced himself as Governor of the "New Netherlands," and named the City and Province New York. Harlem lost some of her inhabitants by abandonment, but others came and occupied their places. Thus ended the Dutch rule. Jan La Montagne (Deputy Sheriff) would not serve under English rule, and threw up his commission. Offenders went unrebuked ; lawlessness was rampant and rum flowed in abundance, causing riots, etc., all about. Nicolls issued orders to the Harlem *Schepens* (magistrates) but they only laughed at him. Finally, Nicolls issued a proclamation, June 12, 1665, putting the city under a Mayor, Alderman and Sheriff, and June 15th the Harlem magistrates were cited to appear before the Council, when there was not so much laughing—they were removed from office. Thomas De Lavall was chosen as Alderman for Harlem, and Resolved Waldron as Constable, the first one in this section. Waldron was authorized to select three or four persons as magistrates, and he named Daniel Tourneur, for Magistrate, and Johannes Vermilia for Court Messenger. Soon after the Governor appointed Tourneur Under Sheriff and President of the offices of *Schout* and *Schepens*. Much trouble arose in the administration of justice in Harlem, owing to the Dutch prejudice against English rule, but in due time "Order reigned in Warsaw."

About this time De Lavall built a grist mill, which was afterwards known as "Mill Camp," mentioned on the "Old Benson Farm." This mill lay a little West of the creek, near 3d avenue. Hage Bruynsen, a Swede, was first miller.

January 13, 1667, the first church, Dutch Reformed, was so far completed that an allotment of seats took place. The ground

upon which the church was built was called *Kerch erf* (church lot).
The *Kerch hof* was the more ancient cemetery, lying in the rear of
the " Judah lot," and may be remembered still as the " Negro
Burying Ground," consisting of one-half acre of land.

The most celebrated resort in Harlem now was Johannes Verveleen's Tavern, near 123d street and 1st Avenue. *Kleyn bier*,
(small beer) Spanish wine and rum were the drinks in those days,
and seemed to be indispensible even at the most trivial business
transaction, and it seems the custom is pretty well kept up in Harlem, except in a change of beverages. One in particular, "40-rod
whiskey," that is the full range at which it is supposed to kill a-
man, if he comes within the circle. I am not a total abstinence
man, but I believe in being temperate in all things ; yet I am con-
strained to say that, in my judgment, at least nine-tenths of the
crimes committed in New York city are either directly or indirectly
traceable to the influences of ardent spirits. I have only to take
the daily criminal records and read them as proof of my assertion.
Many contend that lager beer is not intoxicating. I have tried that
" harmless beverage " myself, and found that it made a hive of
bees in my head and every bee a king ! I heard once of a Holland
bier vendor being put on the witness stand, and he said, " Vell,
I can't swore dat lager ish intoxicating or not, as I tont trinks only
150 classes von tay, und I tont know vat it might too if a man
makesvon hog of hisself!" In Harlem it was a common custom
for even magistrates to have their drinks brought in, while occupying the Bench, and charged to the public expense! Bier and
other beverages were freely used at the ordination of elders and
deacons, and at the performances of funeral solemnities. Families
laid in their bier by half vats (or barrels). Those furnishing bier
at that time were Johannes Vermilye, Dave Verveleen, Isaac De
Forest and Jacob Kipp.

The first Indian trail marked out in Harlem was called " Harlem
Lane," which ran through the " Flats," touched at " McGown's
Pass," through " Clove of the Kill " to North River, and up "Break
neck Hill " to Spuyten Duyvil Creek.

July 15, 1669, the Harlem Ferry was transferred and run by
Johannes Verveleen and called, " From the Island to the Main."

Verveleen settled his ferry on the "Paparinamin," and thus held the key to Manhattan Island. He was constable at Fordham, established a court there and superintended the building of a bridge between Paparinamin and Fordham.

We now come down to 1670, and the only houses now left of the original village of Harlem which I can find here, erected prior to 1670, are two, the "Old Benson House," now occupied as a bathing place, 125th street and Harlem River; and the other the "Van Geisen House," standing partly endwise on 123d Street, between Lexington and Fourth avenues. It was owned by John Kenyon, recently deceased, and is occupied by John H. Covert. It fronted the "Old Boston Stage Road," when it ran by it and up through where now is built, "Harlem Iron Bridge."

August 10, 1673, the Holland and Zealand fleets sailed here and captured "Fort Amsterdam," which they named "Fort William Hendrick," and called New York "New Orange" in honor of Lord Prince of Orange. This was one of the fruits of war now waging in Europe, and Dutch rule was again fully re-established, and Harlem was overjoyed and yielded ready obedience to the new ruler—Anthony Colve as Governor; but it did not last long, for the next year, November 10th, 1674, the province fell again into English hands, and "Fort William Hendrick" was christened "Fort James," and "New Orange" renamed "New York." "The Mayor's Court" was revived, and Sir Edmund Andros became Governor. Although distasteful the English Government was obeyed.

1675 brought fresh alarms, the "King Philip War" commenced in the East, and portended a westward advance with an alliance of all our river Indians. Governor Andros ordered all of the Indian canoes hereabout to be seized and safely confined. He furnished our settlers with arms and ammunition; but the notorious Indian chief being killed August 12th, the war ceased, and quiet again was restored in Harlem.

John Hendricks Brevoort, the well-known ancestor, came to Harlem in 1674.

The ancestor of the Kortright family was Cornelius Jansen—no date of his arrival, but he died in 1689. The main branch of the

Kortrights sprung from Laurens Cornelius Kortright, born here in 1681. They were great land owners.

The Low family sprung from Laurens Jansen, born in Holland, Purchased a lot here of Nicholas De Meyer, in 1662. The present Mayor of Brooklyn, Seth Low, is one of the descendants.

In 1684, the notorious pirate, Captain William Kidd, occupied a portion of this farm with his father-in-law, Captain Samuel Bradley. This farm was located near Hell-gate, and although Kidd was hung, he no doubt occupies a place "down below" similar in name to the one he was removed from!

About this time the city was divided into six wards, Harlem counted as one of the out wards, "embracing all of its farms, plantations and settlements on the island of Manhattan from the north side of the Fresh Water," and divided as formerly, between Harlem and New York, at Saw Mill Creek, and such division to have its local court."

In 1684 Jansen erected the famous tavern, "Half-way House," located on Harlem Lane, at the foot of the hill, about 109th street.

Dominie Selyn, after an absence from Harlem eighteen years, returned and became Pastor of the church.

In 1685, the wolves were as plenty as blackberries, and still destructive on this island, and the city government offered premiums for their annihilation.

In 1686, a new church was projected and built. Laurens Jansen, of the Delamater family, gave his two north seven for the church site. The first stone was laid by Resolved Waldron, the second stone by Johannes Vermilye, and Dominie Selyn preached the first sermon in it. The old bell used in that church is still used in the Dutch Reformed Church at 121st Street and 3d Avenue. It was cast in Holland and contains $20 in gold and $20 in silver, and bears this inscription :—

" Amsterdam, Anno 1734."

" Me Fecit."

This year brought to Harlem Jan Kiersen. He leased " Harlem Heights," called then "Jochem Peters Hills," and built the " Jumel

Mansion," which still remains, and now owned and occupied by
Nelson Chase.

Captain Johannes Benson, the first of the family, came here
purchased a place in Harlem of Peter Van Oblenus, in 1696, and
died in 1715. He was a Dane. The descendants are very
numerous in Harlem, Albany and Schenectady. Samson Benson
Jr., eldest son of Benjamin, inherited the ancestral estate.
From a weakness of his eyes he was called "Crying Sam." His
widow died in 1835, and the estate fell to its sole survivor, Miss
Margaret Benson, who married Andrew McGown, son of Captain
Daniel McGown. The Captain resided then on the north side of
"Church Lane." Captain McGown a Scotch-Irishman, the son
of a clergyman, was the ancestor of the McGown family; he
was lost at sea prior to the Revolution. His widow bought a few
acres on the hill, back of the old Benson Farm, which became
celebrated in the Revolution as "McGown's Pass." Andrew kept
public house, which was part of the Stetson Hotel, called Mount
St. Vincent, and which was burned down in 1881.

Andrew died October 16, 1820. He was the father of Major
Andrew McGown, who participated in the war of 1812, and died
here in 1870. His brother, ex-Alderman Samson B. McGown, aged
85 years, still resides at the old homestead, at 100th Street.
Major McGown was the father of Henry P. McGown, now
occupying the Bench of the 9th Judicial District Civil Court.

I will explain this "McGown's Pass," as it is famous in Revolutionary annals, one of the hardest battles of the Revolution having
been fought there.

This pass was guarded by a block house, built across Harlem
Lane. Col. Miller for eight days held the fort, at "Hoorn's Hook,"
against the British bombardment from the Harlem river, when
they drove him out by firing the fort with hot shot. The
Colonel then retreated with his 300 brave Spartans, Leonidas-like,
and made a brave stand at "McGown's Pass," being surrounded
and attacked by 1500 British and Hessians. It was a desperate
struggle, and was also participated in by General Putnam and
Colonel Knowlton. Colonel Miller's knees were carried away by a
cannon ball, and he expired crying, "AMERICA AND LIBERTY!"

Colonel Knowlton was killed in this battle, which lasted six hours, when the British were completely routed under their commander, Kniphausen. The old block house and the earth works still remain in Central Park as monuments of heroic valor.

An incident occurred near Hell Gate, in 1777, worth relating. A very beautiful girl named Lucy Vanderstine was abducted by a Hessian captain and carried to his camp. Her brother crept softly to the camp at midnight, felled the sentinel, and rescued his sister. He took an oath to kill the first Hessian he should meet with, and did so, soon after, by forcing one of them into a duel. The skull of this Hessian was unearthed on the Dr. Baker farm, at 78th street, a few years ago.

We might allude to the " Jumel Mansion," once more, on Washington Heights, which was once occupied by " the father of his country," in 1776. This house was built by one Phillips, for his daughter Mary, who married Roger Morris. George Washington courted Mary, and came near getting her ; so near, that he would have had her, had Mary consented. National prejudice broke up the match.

It may be well to give some of the Indian names. They called Ward's Island, *Tenkenas* ; Blackwell's Island, *Minnahanonck* ; Spuyten Duyvil Creek, *Shorakapok*, and Hell-gate, *Sewanhacan* (mad waters). The Hollanders called Ward's Island, Great Barent Island, and Rand 's Island, Little Barent Island, and Mount Morris, *Slang Berg*, (Snake Hill.)

One of the Bussing descendants built a dwelling, prior to the Revolution, at McComb's Dam, south side of 8th Avenue, which still remains, and occupied by Charles Francis, a policeman.

Hendrick Van Bramer erected a house, before the Revolution, on the old " Harlem Lane," 7th avenue, between 117th and 118th, streets, which is still standing, and Bartholf occupies it now as a " road house."

Having thus viewed the past, let us dwell briefly, before conclusion, on the present and future of Harlem. It was said by some historian, that Noah, the sole heir of the earth, after the Deluge, gave his acquisitions to his children—to Shem, Asia ; to Ham, (the colored gentleman,) Africa, and to Japhet, Europe. I presume

if he had had a fourth son, America would have been given to him,
or at least that portion of it, called Harlem. What grander or
more beautiful spot can be found than Harlem and its little velvety
islands and silvery rivers, in a golden sunset—sublimely pictur-
esque in vernal bloom—the gorgeous landscape, which charms
every visitor, and fills the mind and soul with rapture.

But a few years ago Harlem was nearly a barren waste—Gold-
smith's " Deserted Village." Everybody was giving it the "shake,"
because it was giving the " shakes " to everybody ! Down-town
people would scarcely come near us, except by the river, because
to cross the Pontine Marshes, or " Harlem Flats," by land, would
squelch the nose of a rhinocerus, and knock the breath out of a
mule ! A balky horse five minutes on the 2d or 3d Avenue railroad track, down there on that Upas desert, would stifle the lungs
of a whole car load, and it was about " which and t'other," as to
which perfume predominated, the natural one from the soil, or
that arising from the covering of it with coal gas tar ! I am told
that aquatic excursionists found it safer to burn brimstone as they
came up through Hell-gate ! It has been filled in since, and soon
will be built over. At the commencement of the Rebellion (1861)
Harlem began to grow, and few parts of our city have grown faster
and been more beautified by new buildings, than this. New settlers are constantly arriving, trade is spreading on every street and
avenue, and everybody says they are happy and making money,
excepting the Elevated Railroad ! In this connection, and to con-
trast travel with the past, I might mention the first stage, in 1832,
which run from Wm. D. Bradshaw's corner, (now Marsh's Drug
Store) in Harlem, to down town. Soon after, the " Franklin " run
from Harlem to Pell street and the Bowery—fare fifty cents the
round trip. Now, some grumble at ten cents on the Elevated
railroad, and get angry because they don't let 'em carry along a
small grocery store in the bargain. Up to 1843 only seven stages
were on the road. In 1853 the 3d avenue horse railroad was
chartered, which took twice as long to ride down town as in the
stages—an hour and twenty minutes, providing no horse balked
or fell dead across the track.

The Elevated makes now about four trips to one of the surface,

and yet the surface roads are doing a better business than ever.
The Harlem Navigation Line, from Harlem to Peck Slip in half an
hour, came in as a relief prior to the elevated convenience. The
Elevated Railroad, by its connecting links on the East and West
sides, has made Harlem, enriched property owners, increased trade,
lowered the prices of produce and merchandise, but raised rents.
Landlords, go slow on that; our people will not stand too much
imposition. I am glad to see our tradesmen try to please their
customers by competing with down town merchants. It is better
for the purchaser to leave his money in Harlem and the vender to
secure it here by fair dealing. I don't think the ladies consider
the importance of home trading so much as they do the pleasure of
down-town shopping. Many is the time they want a paper of nee-
dles, then on with the bonnet and away on "rapid transit" to Macy's,
or Stewart's, or Taylor's I knew a lady last summer, who wanted a
certain kind of mitts and could get them down town for forty cents,
ten cents less than the same kind here. She purchased, came home;
forty cents for mitts and twenty cents for car fare, total sixty cents.
Next day she went down and changed them. For mitts, car fare
and lunch, one dollar and five cents—out by not trading here, fifty-
five cents. That is tightening the spigot and loosing out of the
bung. I certainly must commend the spirit and enterprise of our
Harlem tradesmen now. Not to be invidious, but I am sure you
can trade now in nearly all things as cheap in Harlem as elsewhere;
so go and buy your piano from Behning, who makes the best
pianos now in use; your dry goods of such firms as Callan
and others; your clothing of Stone & Goodman, or the Harlem and
Westchester Clothing House; your groceries of William
Robinson, Ayers, or Bennett & Jarvis; your shoes of the
Zabinskies, Goodman, or your furniture of George Fennell
& Company and Anthony Brothers; your carpets of Croft
Brothers; your hardware of Charles Mann or Dickerman;
your Millinery of Piser or Madden & McGlinn; your fancy
goods of Williams & Co., Spier, or Holmes; your gent's furnish-
ing goods of Hartley; your stationary and such nicknacks of
Phillips, Goddard, or Speck; your jewelry of Gleason, Keeping;
your Foreign and Domestic delicacies of Lazarus & Stender; your

hats of Kelly or Goldsmid; all kinds of sewing machines of Raaech; your rubber goods of Goodyear, and others, and you will save time and money, and aid our tradesmen by quick sales to compete with down-town traffic.

The "Harlem River Improvement," so long and so much talked about, must necessarily be consummated in about two years. Congressman Flower recently had passed an appropriation of $50,000. A commission has in charge the settlement of compensation to the land-owners along the Fac, and their duty is nearly ended, while General Newton reports that his surveys will soon be done; and I see no reason now why the great artificial channel, or ship canal, cannot go forward to completion, thus comingling the waters of the Hudson, Harlem and East Rivers with those of the sea, and circle Harlem's borders with one of the finest marts in the known world. Think of the immense cargoes of all kinds of merchandise which will come through this way instead of going as usual around the Battery, sixteen miles further. The cost of this enterprise is estimated between three and four millions. The channel will be four hundred feet wide, eighteen feet deep, and six miles long, starting from Randall's Island, running through Dyckman,s meadows, and terminating at the Hudson River and mouth of Spuyten Duyvil Creek. It is also proposed to deepen the channel of the Harlem Kills, and thus make a direct connection between Harlem and the Sound, and avoid the dangerous passage of Hell Gate. When this great work shall have been completed, the vessels of every clime will surround Harlem, our streets will be thronged with the busy life of a Broadway, and this famous old Dutch town will be the grand commercial centre of the metropolis! With what delight the first settler of Harlem, Kuyter, would then, if alive, look upon the scene in contrast with his beloved *Zegendal* of 400 acres, 228 years ago! also, if the old Hollander, Gov. William Kieft, could then rise from the vasty deep, where he went down with the ship Princess, and gaze upon Harlem, wherein he gave so many grants and ground briefs, his heart would leap with rapture, and, in his usual jolly mood, he would say, "Come in goot frients and trink wine 'New Amsterdam peer.'" Who among us then, with Harlem's past history before you, and the goodly prospects in store, are not proud of being called Harlemites? Let us cultivate the friendship as of yore, in " ye ancient village," and leave animosities and contentions to other localities; and though we may differ scientifically, politically, and even religiously, let us unite cordially and friendly, in every public and private business enterprise which may have a tendency to progress, build up, and benefit our own beloved HARLEM.

APPENDIX.

EARLY HISTORY OF NEW YORK, FROM 1598 TO 1674.
COMPILED AND ARRANGED FROM
AUTHENTIC SOURCES.

It is a mistaken idea that Hendrick Hudson made the first landing on New York Island, or "Island of Manhattan," in 1609, as some historians have it. The earliest records extant state that as early as 1598, a few Hollanders, in the employ of a Greenland Company, were in the habit of resorting to New Netherlands (i. e. New York), not, it is true, with a design of effecting a settlement, but merely to secure a shelter during the winter months. With this view they built two small forts, to protect themselves against the Indians. Nevertheless, the fact remains undisputed, that to Hudson belongs the honor of being the first one who directed public attention to the Island of Manhattan as an advantageous point for a trading port in the New World.

On the 4th of April, 1609, the great navigator sailed out of the harbor of Amsterdam, and "by twelve of ye clocke" of the 6th he was two leagues off the land. He was in the employ of the Dutch East India Company, who had commissioned him to seek a passage to the East Indies by the north side of Nova Zembla. Having, however, found the sea at that part full of ice, he turned the prow of his little vessel, the *Half-Moon*, westward, and, after a month's cruise, reached the great Bank of Newfoundland, on the 2d of July. Thence he sailed southward to the James River, Virginia, and again altering his course—still in pursuit of a new channel to India—he coasted along the shores of New Jersey, and on the 2d of September, 1609, cast anchor inside of Sandy Hook.

Hudson, having explored the river that bears his name as far as the present City of Albany, set sail on the 4th of October for Europe, bearing the news of the discovery of a new country—the opening for the new *commerce*; for although his patrons were disappointed in finding a short road to the land of silks, teas, and spices, still, his great discovery was destined to open in future time mines of wealth, more valuable than all the imagined riches of the Celestial Empire.

At that period, Holland carried on a lucrative trade with the East Indies and Russia. Every year they dispatched nearly one hundred ships to Archangel for furs; but Hudson's glowing accounts of the rich peltry he had seen in the newly discovered regions soon turned the attention of the busy Dutch to a country where these articles could be purchased without the taxes of custom-houses and other duties. Accordingly, in the year 1610, a few merchants dispatched another vessel, under the command of the *Half-Moon's* former mate, to traffic in furs with the Indians. This venture met with such success, that two years after, in 1612, the *Fortune* and the *Tiger*, commanded, respectively, by Hendrick Christiaensen and Adrien Block, sailed on a trading voyage to the "Mauritius River," as the Hudson was first named. The following year, also, three more vessels, commanded by Captains De Witt, Volckertsen, and Wey, sailed from Amsterdam and Hoven on a similar adventure. These were the beginnings of the important fur trade which was, ere long, to be a chief source of wealth to Holland and America. It was now determined to open a regular communication with the newly-discovered region, and to make the Island of Manhattan the depot of the fur trade in America. It was also resolved to establish permanent agents here for the purchase and collection of skins, while the vessels were on their voyages to and from Holland. Captain Hendrick Christiaensen became the first agent, and built a redoubt, with four small houses, on ground which, it is said, is now the site of No. 39 Broadway.

A little navy was commenced about the same period, by Captain Adrien Block, one of the vessels of which was accidentally burned, just on the eve of his departure for Holland. Having abundant materials, however, in the Island of Manhattan, he finished another; and in the spring of 1614, launched the first vessel ever built in New Amsterdam. She was named the *Restless*, a yacht of sixteen tons—a name prophetic of the ever-busy and future great city. The entire winter passed in building the vessel, the Indians kindly supplying the strangers with food. Such were the earliest movements of commerce in New Netherlands about 284 years ago.

A few months before Captain Block's return to Holland, the States-General of the Netherlands, with a view of encouraging emigration, passed an ordinance granting the discoverers of new countries the exclusive privilege of trading at Manhattan during four voyages. Accordingly, the merchants who had sent out the first expedition had a map made of all the country between Canada and Virginia, as the whole new region was called, and claiming to be the original discoverers, petitioned the Government for the promised monopoly. Their petition was granted; and on the 11th of October, 1614, they obtained a charter for the exclusive right of the trade on the territory within the 40th and 45th degrees of north latitude. The charter also forbade all other persons to interfere with this monopoly, in the penalty of confiscating both vessels and cargoes, with a fine also of 50,000 Dutch ducats for the benefit of the charter's grantees. The new province first formally received the name of *New Netherland* in this document; and Dutch merchants, associating themselves under the name of the "United New Netherland Company," straightway prepared to conduct their operations on a more extensive scale. Trading parties in the interior hastened to collect furs from the Indians, and deposit them at Fort Nassau (Albany) and Manhattan. Jacob Eelkins, a shrewd trader, received the appointment of agent at the former place, where the first one, Captain Christiaensen, had been murdered by an Indian. This was the first murder ever recorded in the new province.

In the year 1617, a formal treaty of peace and alliance was concluded between the Dutch and the powerful nation of the Iroquois. The pipe of peace was smoked, and the hatchet buried in the earth, on the present site of Albany.

Trade became so profitable, that when the charter of the United New Netherland Company expired, in 1618, they petitioned for a renewal, but failing to obtain it they continued their trade two or three years longer, under a special cense.

Up to this period, the Hollanders had considered Manhattan as a trading post only, and dwelt in mere temporary huts of rude construction. But the British now explored the American coast, claiming the whole region between Canada and Virginia, and from the Atlantic to the Pacific Oceans; and the Dutch, consequently began to realize the importance of securing the American possessions in the new province. The English Puritans, hearing glowing accounts of the New Netherland, requested permission to emigrate there with their families. But the States-General, having other plans in view, declined the prayers of the Puritans. They thought it better policy to supply the new province with their own countrymen, and on the third of June, 1621, granted a charter to the West India Company for twenty years, which conferred upon them the exclusive jurisdiction over New Netherland. Meanwhile, the Puritans, not disheartened, reached Plymouth Rock, and thus conveyed their faith and traffic to the shores of New England, where they continue to this day.

The West India Company now began to colonize the new province with fresh zeal. The Amsterdam Chamber, in 1623, fitted out a ship of 250 tons, the *New Netherland*, in which thirty families embarked for the distant territory whose name she bore. Captain Wey commanded the expedition, having been appointed the first Director of the province. Most of the colonists were *Walloons*, or French Protestants, from the borders of France and Belgium and sought a home from religious persecutions in their own land.

With the arrival of the *New Netherland*, a new era in the domestic history of the settlement began. Soon saw-mills supplied the necessary timber for comfortable dwellings, in the place of the bark-huts built after the Indian fashion. The new buildings were generally one-story high, with two rooms on a floor, and a thatched roof garret. From the want of brick and mortar, the chimneys were constructed of wood. The interior was, as a matter of course, very scantily supplied with furniture—the great chest from *Fatherland*, with its prized household goods, being the most imposing article. Tables were generally the heads of barrels placed on end, rough shelves constituted the cupboard, and chairs were logs of wood rough hewn from the forest. To complete the furniture, there was the well known ' *Sluap Banck*," or sleeping-bench—the bedstead—where lay the boast, the pride, the comfort of a Dutch housekeeper, the feather bed. Around the present Battery and Coenties Slip and the Bowling-Green were the houses, a few of which were surrounded by gardens. The fruit-trees often excited the thievish propensities of the natives, and one devastating war followed the shooting of an Indian girl while stealing peaches from an orchard on Broadway, near the present Bowling Green. Meanwhile commerce kept pace with the new houses, and the staunch ship, the *New Netherland*, returned to Holland with a cargo of furs valued at $12,000.'

Anxious to fulfil its part of the agreement, the West India Company in 1625, also sent to Manhattan three ships and a yacht, containing a number of families, armed with farming implements, and 103 head of cattle. Fearing the cattle might be lost in the surrounding forests, the settlers landed them on Nutten's (Governor's) Island, but afterward conveyed them to Manhattan. Two more vessels shortly after arrived from Holland, and the settlement soon numbered some 200 persons, and gave promise of permanency.

In the year 1624, Wey, returning to Holland, William Verhulst succeeded him in the Directorship. The latter, however, did not long enjoy the emoluments of office, for at the end of the year he also was recalled, and Peter Minuit appointed, in his place. Director-General of New Netherland, with full power to organize a provisional government. He arrived May 4, 1626, in the ship *Seaman*, Adrian Jovis, captain. The first seal was now granted to the province, having for a crest, a beaver, than which, for a coat of arms, nothing could have been more appropriate. It was fitting that the earliest Hollanders of the "Empire City" should thus honor the animal that was so fast enriching them in their newly-adopted home.

To the credit of Director Minuit, be it said, the very first act of his administration was to purchase in an open and honorable manner the Island of Manhattan from the Indians for sixty gilders, or twenty-four dollars. The Island itself was estimated to contain 22,000 acres. The price paid, it is true, was a mere trifle, but the purchase itself was lawful and satisfactory to the aboriginal owners—a fact which cannot be truly said in regard to other regions taken from the Indians.

To assist him in carrying out his instructions, the Director was furnished with an Executive Council. The latter was, in turn, assisted by the *Koopman*, who acted as Secretary to the province and book-keeper of the public warehouse. Last of all, came the *Schout-Fiscal*, a civil factotum, half sheriff and attorney-general, executive officer of the Council, and general custom-house official. Thus early had the Dutch an eye to the "main chance," the export of furs that year (1626) amounting to $19,000, and giving promise of a constant increase.

Some thirty rudely constructed log-houses now extended along the shores of the East River, and these, with a block-house, a horse-mill, and a "Company's" thatched stone building, constituted the settlement of the present City of New York. Clergyman or schoolmaster was as yet unknown in the infant colony. Every settler had his own cabin and cows, tilled his land or traded with the Indians—all were busy, like their own emblem, the beaver.

In the year 1629, the "Charter of Privileges and Exemptions" was granted in Holland, and *patroons* were allowed to settle in the new colony. This important document transferred to the free soil of America the old feudal tenure and burdens of Continental Europe. The proposed *Patrooneries* were only transcripts of the *Seigneuries* and *Lordships* so common at that period, and which the French were, at the same time, establishing in Canada. In that province, even at the present day, the feudal appendages of jurisdiction, pre-emption rights, monopolies of mines, minerals and waters, with hunting, fishing and fowling, form a part of the civil law. Pursuing, however, a more liberal policy, the grantees of the charter to the New Netherland *patroons* secured the Indian's right to his native soil, at the same time enjoining schools and churches.

Meanwhile, the settlement in New Netherland continued to prosper, and soon became the principal depot for the fur and coasting trade of the *patroons*. The latter were obliged to land all their cargoes at Fort Amsterdam : and in the years 1629-30, the imports from old Amsterdam amounted to 113,000 gailders, and the exports from Manhattan exceeded 130,000. The Company reserved the exclusive right to the fur trade, and imposed a duty of five per cent, on all the trade of the *patroons*.

The inhabitants, in order not to be idle, turned their attention, with fresh zeal, to ship-building, and with so much success, that as early as 1631, New Amsterdam had become the metropolis of the New World. The *New Netherlands*, a ship of 800 tons, was built at Manhattan, and dispatched to Holland—an important event of the times, since the vessel was one of the largest merchantmen of the world. It was a very costly experiment, however, and was not soon repeated. Emigrants from all nations now began to flock into the new colony. They were principally induced to come by the liberal offers of the Dutch Company, who transported them in its own vessels at the cheap rate of twelve and a half cents *per diem* passage and stores ; giving them, also, as a still further inducement, as much land as they could cultivate. Nor were those the only reasons which caused them to leave their *Fatherland*. With a wise and liberal policy, totally different from that of its eastern neighbors, the Dutch granted the fullest religious toleration. The Walloons, Calvinists, Quakers, Catholics and Jews, all found a safe and religious home in the New Netherland, and here laid the broad and solid foundation of that tolerant character ever since retained by the City of New York. In our streets and along our broad avenues may be seen on any Sabbath, Jews, Gentiles and Christians, all worshiping God in their sacred temples, and " according to the dictates of their own conscience."

In the same year (1632), Peter Minuit, the Director, it will be remembered, of New Netherland, was suspected of favoring the *patroons*, and was recalled from his Directorship. He returned to Holland in the ship *Eendragt* (which had brought over his dismissal), which carried also, a return cargo of 5,000 beaver-skins—an evidence of the colony's commercial prosperity. The vessel, driven by stress of weather, put into the harbor of Plymouth, where she was retained, on the ground of having illegally interfered with English monopolies. This arrest of the Dutch trader led to a correspondence between the rival powers, in which the respective claims of each were distinctly set forth. The Hollanders claimed the following grounds : 1st. Its discovery by them in the year 1609 ; 2d. The return of their people in 1610 ; 3d. The grant of a trading charter in 1614 ; 4th. The maintenance of a fort, until 1621, when the West India Company was organized ; and, 5th. Their purchase of the land from the Indians. The English, on the contrary, defended their right of possession from the prior discovery of Cabot and the patent of James I. to the Plymouth Company. The Indians, they argued, as wanderers, were not the *bona fide* owners of the land, and hence, had no right to it, consequently, their titles must be invalid. But England, being at this period just on the eve of a civil war, was in no condition to force her claims; and she, therefore, having released the *Eendragt*, contented herself with the mere assumption of authority—reserving the accomplishment of her designs until a more convenient season.

At length, in the month of April, 1633, the ship *Southberg* reached Manhattan with Wouter Van Twiller, the new Director-General (or Governor), and a military force of one hundred and four soldiers, together with a Spanish caravel, captured on the way. Among the passengers, also came Dominie Everardus Bogardus and Adam Roolansen, the first regular clergyman and schoolmaster to New Amsterdam. A church now became indispensable ; and a room over the horse-mill, where prayers had been regularly read for seven years, was abandoned for a rude wooden church, on Pearl, between Whitehall and Froid streets, on the shore of the East River. This was the first Reformed Dutch Church in the city ; and near by were constructed the parsonage and the Dominie's stables. The graveyard was laid out on Broadway in the vicinity of Morris street.

Van Twiller occupied " Farm No. 1" of the Company, which extended from Wall to Hudson street. " Farm No. 3," at Greenwich, he appropriated as his tobacco plantation. The new Governor and the Dominie did not harmonize. Bogardus had interfered in public concerns, which Van Twiller resented, the former, from his pulpit, pronounced the Governor a " Child of Satan." This, doubtless, was very true, but the "Child of Satan " became so incensed, as never to enter the church door again. Early times had their own peculiar ways of doing things, the same as ourselves. In 1638, " for slandering the Rev. E. Bogardus," an old record states, " a woman was obliged to appear at the sound of a bell, in the fort, before the Governor and Council, and say that she knew he was honest and pious, and that she had lied falsely."

Van Twiller had been promoted from a clerkship in the Company's Warehouse, and seems to have been a very incompetent Governor. He probably obtained the place, not from fitness, but from the same means which act in similar cases at the present day, viz: political influence, arising from the fact that he had married the daughter of Killian Van Rensselaer, the wealthy *patroon*.

The Company had authorized him to fortify the depots of the fur trade. Accordingly, the fort on the Battery, commenced in the year 1626, was rebuilt, and a guard-house and barracks prepared for the soldiers. Several brick and stone dwellings were erected within the fort, and three windmills, used to grind the grain for the garrison, on the southwest bastion of the fort. African slaves were the laborers principally engaged upon these improvements. At a subsequent period, when these slaves had grown old, they petitioned the authorities for their freedom, and recounted their services at the time mentioned in support of their application, in proof of which they presented a certificate given them by their overseer : "That during the administration of Van Twiller, he (Jacob Stoffelsen), as overseer of the Company's negroes, was continually employed with said negroes in the construction of Fort Amsterdam, which was finished in 1635 ; and that the negroes assisted in chopping trees for the big house, making and splitting palisades, and other work." The "big house" here referred to was the Governor's residence. It was built of brick, and was, no doubt, a substantial edifice, as it is found to have served for the residence of successive chiefs of the colony during the whole of the Dutch era, and for a few years subsequent.

In respect to the walls of the fort, they were in no wise improved by the incompetent Van Twiller, except the northwest bastion, which was faced with stone. The other parts of the walls were simply banks of earth without ditches; nor were they even surrounded by a fence to keep off the goats and animals running wild in the town. When Governor Kieft arrived, in 1638, as Van Twiller's successor, he found the fort in a decayed state, "opening on every side, so that nothing could obstruct going in or coming out, except at the stone point." Nevertheless, there is no doubt that the fort exercised a very salutary influence in keeping the Indians at a respectful distance.

In 1633, the commercial importance of New Amsterdam was increased by the grant of the "Staple Right," a sort of feudal privilege similar to the *Fatherland*. By it, all vessels trading along the coast, or sailing on the rivers, were obliged to either discharge their cargoes at the port, or pay certain duties. This soon became a valuable right, as it gave to New Amsterdam the commercial monopoly of the whole Dutch province.

A short time before the arrival of Governor Van Twiller, De Vries, whose little colony at Snalenduel, Delaware had been cut off by the Indians, returned to America on a visit, in the mammoth ship, *New Netherland*. A yacht, about this time, also arrived—the English ship, *William*, with Jacob Eelkins, who had been dismissed as supercargo by the Company, in 1632. Enraged by this dismissal, he had entered the service of the English, and had now returned to promote their interests in the fur trade on the Mauritius (Hudson) River.

This was a bold act, and contrary to the policy of the West India Company. Accordingly, Van Twiller, who, though an inefficient Governor, was a thorough merchant, and understood the important monopoly of the fur trade, refused permission for the vessel to proceed further on its way. His demand upon Eelkins for his commission was refused by the latter, on the ground that he occupied British territory, and would sail up the river at the cost, if need be, of his life. Thereupon, the Director, ordering the national flag to be hoisted, and three guns to be fired in honor of the Prince of Orange, forbade him to proceed further in the name of his master, the Dutch Government.

But, far from being daunted by this prohibition, Eelkins answered by running up, in his turn, the British colors, firing a salute for King Charles, and coolly steered up the river in defiance of Fort Amsterdam. The amazement of Van Twiller at the audacity of the ex-Dutch agent may be easily imagined. Astonished as he was at this daring act, the Director, nevertheless, proceeded very philosophically: First, he summoned all the people to the front of the fort, now the Bowling Green; next he ordered a cask of wine, and another of beer; then, filling his own glass, he called on all good citizens who loved the Prince of Orange to follow his patriotic example, and drink confusion to the English Government. The people, of course, were not slow in obeying this reasonable request; indeed, what more could they do, for the English ship was now far beyond all reach, safely pursuing her way up the Hudson. Still, while they drank his wine, they were deeply mortified at the Governor's cowardice. De Vries openly charged him with it, and plainly told him, if it had been his case, he should have sent some "eight-pound beans" after the impudent Englishman, and helped him down the river again; but it being now too late to do this, he should send the *Southberg* after him and drive him down the river. The effect of this advice was not lost upon the Governor, for a few days after, Van Twiller screwed up his courage sufficiently to dispatch an armed force to Fort Orange (Albany), where Eelkins had pitched his tent, and where he found he was busily engaged in trading with the Indians. The Dutch soldiers quickly destroyed his canvas store, and, re-shipping the goods, brought the vessel back to Fort Amsterdam. Eelkins was then required to give up his peltry; after which, he was sent to sea, with the warning never again to interfere with the Dutch Government trade.

Meanwhile the settlement at Fort Amsterdam—the New York embryo—continued to increase and prosper, men of enterprise and wealth often arriving. Most of these came from the Dutch Netherlands, and thus transferred the domestic economy and habits of Holland and the Rhine to the banks of the Hudson. Ships were loaded with bricks burned in Holland, and, at first, every dwelling was modeled after those they had left, and with store-rooms for trade, like those of Amsterdam and other trading towns in *Fatherland.* Thus, at New Amster dam and Fort Orange (Albany), rows of houses could be seen built of imported brick, with thatched roofs, wooden chimnies, and their gable ends always toward the street. Inside were all the neatness, frugality, order and industry which the inmates brought from their native land. Until the year 1652, city streets and lots were unknown, adventurers and settlers selecting land wherever most convenient for their purpose. Hence the crooked courses of some of our down-town streets.

Cornelius Drecken owned a farm by the present Peck Slip, and ferried passengers across the East River for the small sum of three stivers, in *wampum.* At that time, Pearl street formed the bank of the river. Water, Front, and South streets have all been reclaimed for the purpose of increasing trade and commerce. The old wooden, *shingled house*, one of the last venerable relics of the olden time, on the corner of Peck Slip, was so near the river that a stone could be easily thrown into it. Pearl, it is thought, was the first street occupied, the first houses being built here in 1633. Bridge street came next; and a deed is still in existence for a lot on it, thirty-four by one hundred and ten feet, for the sum of twenty-four guilders, or nine dollars and sixty cents. This is the earliest conveyance of city property on record. Whitehall, Stone, Broad, Beaver and Marketfield were opened soon after. In the year 1642, the first grant of a city lot, east of the fort at the Battery, was made by Hendrickson Rip. During the next year, several lots were granted on the lower end of "Heese Straat," as Broadway was then named. Martin Krigier was the first grantee of a lot of land in this section, opposite the

Bowling Green, which contained eighty-six rods. Then he built the well-known "Krieger's Tavern," which soon became a fashionable resort.

At this critical moment, the third Division-General and Governor, arrived March, 1638, as the successor of the weak Van Twiller. His first step was to organize a Council, retaining, however, its entire control. Dr. Johannes L. Montagne, a learned Huguenot, was appointed by him a member of this new board. Cornelius Van Tienhoven, from Utrecht, one of the oldest settlers, was appointed Colonial Secretary, with a salary of two hundred and fifty dollars *per annum*; while Ulrich Leopold continued as School-Fiscal, or Sheriff and Attorney-General. Adrian Dircksen was made Assistant Commissary, because he spoke correctly the language of the Mohawks, and was "well versed in the art of trading with them." The Rev. Mr. Bogardus continued the Dominie, and Adam Roolausen the Schoolmaster.

The new Governor did not confine himself to correcting *official* abuses solely : he issued, also, proclamations to improve the *moral* condition of the settlement, and all persons were seriously enjoined from "fighting and all other immoralities," as the guilty would be punished, and made a terror to all evil-doers. Rightly judging, also, that public worship would be a peaceful auxiliary to his labors, and the old wooden church of Van Twiller having fallen to pieces, he determined to erect a new one inside the fort. Jochem Pietersen, Kuyter, Jan Jansen Dauen, with Kieft and Captain Vries, as "Kirke Meesters," superintended the new work, and John and Richard Ogden were the masons. The building was of stone, seventy-two by fifty-two feet, and sixteen high, and cost 2,500 guilders : its legend, translated from the Dutch, read : Anno Domini, 1642, Wilhelm Kieft, Director-General, both the Community caused to build this temple." New Amsterdam had a town bell ; this was now removed to the belfry of the new church, whence it regulated the city movements, the time for laborers, the courts, merry wedding peals, tolled the funerals, and called the people to the Lord's House.

Hardly, however, had Kieft got his plans for the moral reformation of his people fairly under way, when, as before hinted, the *patroons* began to give fresh trouble ; that class now (1638) demanded "new privileges"—"that they might monopolize more territory—be invested with the largest feudal powers, and enjoy free trade throughout New Netherland." Nor was this all. In their arrogance they also demanded that all "private persons" and poor emigrants should not be allowed to purchase lands from the Indians, but should settle within the colonies under the jurisdiction of the manorial lords—*i. e. themselves.*

These grasping demands of the *patroons* were reserved for future consideration by the States-General : and it was determined to try free competition in the Internal trade of the New Netherland. A notification was accordingly published in the Amsterdam Chamber, that all the inhabitants of the United Provinces, and of friendly countries, might convey to New Netherland, "in the Company's ships," any cattle and merchandise, and might "receive whatever returns they or their agents were able to obtain in those quarters therefor." A duty of ten per cent. was paid to the Company on all goods exported from New Netherland with the freight. Every emigrant, upon his arrival at New Amsterdam, was to receive "as much land as he and his family could properly cultivate. This liberal system gave a great impulse to the prosperity of New Netherland by encouraging emigration of substantial colonists, but only from Holland, not from Virginia and New England. *Conscience* had ever been free in New Netherland, and now trade and commerce were also made free to all. Political franchise in Massachusetts was limited to church members, and now "many men began to enquire after the Southern ports," not from the climate there, or the necessary wants of life, but, in the language of the old chronicler, " to escape their insupportable government." The only obligation required of emigrants was an oath of fidelity and allegiance to the colony, the same as imposed upon the Dutch settlers. Both parties enjoyed equal privileges.

In 1640, Director Kieft determined upon another unwise measure, viz: the exaction of a contribution, a tax of corn, furs and *wampum*, from the Indians about Fort Amsterdam. This and other improper acts entirely estranged them from the settlers, and laid the foundation of bloody war, which, the next year, (1641), desolated New Netherland. Meanwhile, Kieft continuing stubborn, sent sloops to Tappan to levy contributions; but the natives indignantly refused to pay the novel tribute. In their own plain language, they wondered how the Sachem at the fort dared to exact such things from them. He must be, they said, a very shabby fellow; he had come to live on their land, where they had not invited him, and now came to deprive them of their corn for no equivalent.

Notwithstanding, however, the many injudicious acts of Governor Kieft, it cannot be denied that, during his administration, the trade of New Amsterdam began to be better regulated. The streets of the town also, were better laid out in the lower section of the city. In 1641, Kieft instituted two annual fairs, for the purpose of encouraging agriculture; one of which was held in October, for cattle, and the other the next month, for hogs, upon the Bowling Green. The holding of these fairs opened the way for another important addition to the comfort of the town. No tavern, as yet, had been started in the Dutch settlement; and the numerous visitors from the interior and the New England colonies had to avail themselves of the Governor's hospitalities. The fairs increasing in number, Kieft found them a heavy tax upon his politeness, as well as his larder; and, in 1642, he erected a large, stone tavern at the Company's expense. It was situated on a commanding spot, near the present Coenties Slip, and was afterwards altered into the " *Stadt Huys*," or City Hall.

About this time the increasing intercourse and business with the English settlements made it necessary that more attention should be paid to the English language. Governor Kieft had, it is true, some knowledge of the English tongue; but his subordinates were generally ignorant of it- a circumstance which often caused great embarrassment. George Baxter was accordingly appointed his English Secretary, with a salary of two hundred dollars *per annum;* and thus, for the first time, the English language was officially recognized in New Amsterdam.

The first charter of New Netherland restricted, as we have seen, the commercial privileges of the *Patroons;* but in the year 1640, they wereextended to " all free colonists," and the stockholders in the Dutch Company. Nevertheless the latter body adhered to onerous imports, for its own benefit, and required a duty of ten per cent. on all goods shipped to New Netherland and five upon return cargoes, excepting peltry, which paid ten at Manhattan before exported. The prohibition of manufactures within the province was now abolished, and the Company renewed its promise to send over " as many blacks as possible "

In 1643 the colonists easily obtained goods from the Company's warehouse, whither they were obliged to bring their fur purchases, before shipment to Holland. The furs were then generally sold at Amsterdam, under the supervision of a *patroon*, whose share first was one-half, but was afterwards reduced one-sixth. Under this system, the price of a beaver skin, which before 1642 had been six, now rose to ten " fathoms."

In 1644, the ever-busy New Englander—imagining that the beavers came from " a great lake in the northwest part " of their patent—began to covet a share in the fur trade on the Delaware. Accordingly an expedition was despatched from Boston to " sail up the Delaware as high as they could go; and some of the company, under the conduct of Mr. William Aspinwall, a good artist, and one who had been in those parts, to pass by small skiffs and canoes up the river, so far as they could."

This continued interference of New England adventurers with the Delaware trade, at length became very annoying to Kieft, as well as to Printz, the Swedish Governor of the Delaware colony. The Dutch at New Amsterdam, as the earliest explorers of the South River, had seen their trading monopoly there invaded by the Swedes; but the New Englanders made their appearance in pursuit of the same prize, the Swedes had common cause with the Dutch to repel the new intruders. The question of sovereignty was soon raised abroad by the arrival of two ships, the *Key of Calmar* and *Flame*, sent home by Printz with large cargoes of tobacco and beaver-skins. Bad weather, and the war just begun between Denmark and Sweden, made three vessels run into the Port of Harlington in Friesland. There they were seized by the West India Company, which both claimed sovereignty over all the regions around the South River and exacted the import duties that their charter granted it. The Swedish minister at the Hague protested against these exactions, and a long correspondence ensued, which resulted in the vessels being discharged the following summer upon payment of the import duties.

During the year 1644, Kieft, headstrong and imprudent as usual, became involved in a war with the New England Indians. At this juncture of affairs, a ship arrived from Holland with a cargo of goods for Van Rensselaer's *patroonery*, and Kieft, the Dutch forces being in want of clothing, called upon the supercargo to furnish fifty pairs of shoes for the soldiers, offering full payment in silver, beavers, or *seawan*. The supercargo, however, zealously regarding his *patroon's* mercantile interests, refused to comply, whereupon the Governor ordered a levy, and obtained enough shoes to supply as many soldiers as afterward killed five hundred of the enemy. The Governor, much provoked, next commanded the vessel to be thoroughly searched, when a large lot of guns and ammunition, not in the manifest, were declared contraband, and the ship and cargo confiscated. Winthrop says that he had on board 4,000 weight of powder and seven hundred pieces to trade with the natives. For such acts as these, Kieft seems to have been equally detested by both Indians and Dutch, the former desiring his removal, and daily crying, " Wouter ! Wouter ?" meaning Wouter Van Twiller, his immediate predecessor.

Meanwhile, the Indian war continued; the Dutch settlers were in danger of utter destruction, and the expenses of the soldiery could not be met. Neither could the West India Company send aid to its unfortunate colony, as that body had been made bankrupt by its military operations in Brazil. A bill of exchange, drawn by Kieft upon the Amsterdam Chamber, came back protested. The demands for public money were too pressing to await the slow proceedings of the Admiralty Court. Accordingly, soon after this, on the 29th of May, 1644, a privateer, the *La Garse*, Captain Blauvelt, having been commissioned by the Governor to cruise in the West Indies, returned to Manhattan with two rich Spanish prizes.

About this time the ship *Blue Cock* arrived from Curacoa with one hundred and thirty Dutch soldiers, quite a relief to the New Netherlanders against their savage foe.

At length the pitiable condition of the New Netherland colony attracted the attention of the Dutch Government. Its originators, as before mentioned, had become nearly, if not entirely, bankrupt.

To use their own official words, " the long-looked-for profits thence " had not arrived, and they themselves had no means to relieve " the poor inhabi-

tants who had left the *Fatherland;*" accordingly, the bankrupt Company
urged the "States-General" for a subsidy of 1,600,000 of guilders to place the
Dutch province in a good, prosperous and profitable order.

This body directed observations to be made into the affairs of New Netherland, and also into the propriety of restricting its internal trade to residents,
with the policy of opening a free one between Brazil and Manhattan. Upon
making this investigation, it was found that New Netherland, instead of becoming a source of commercial profit to the Company, had absolutely cost
that body, from the year 1626 to 1644, "over 550,000 guilders, deducting returns received from there." Still, "the Company cannot decently or consist-
ently abandon it." The Director's salary, the report continues, should be
3,600 guilders, and the whole civil and military establishment of New Netherland, 20,000 guilders. As many African negroes, it thought, should be brought
from Brazil as the *patroons,* farmers and settlers " would be willing to pay for
at a fair price." It would thus appear that our Dutch forefathers had something to do with the slave trade as well as the Southern colonies. Free grants
of land should be granted to all emigrants on Manhattan Island, a trade
allowed to Brazil and the fisheries; the manufacture and exportation of salt
should be encouraged, and the duties of "revenue officers be sharply attended
to." Such was the business condition of the New Netherland in the year 1645.
The five previous years of Indian wars had hardly known five months of peace
and prosperity. Kieft, perceiving his former errors, now concluded a treaty
of amity with the Indians, August 30, 1645. In two years, 1,600 savages had
been killed at Manhattan and its neighborhood, and scarcely one hundred
could be found besides traders.

Soon after the peace, in 1647, Kieft, having been recalled, embarked for
Holland, carrying with him specimens of the New Netherland minerals (gath-
ered by the Raritan Indians in the Neversink Hills), and a fortune, which his
enemies estimated at 100,000 guilders. Dominie Bogardus and Van der Huy-
gens, late Fiscal, were fellow-passengers in the richly laden vessel. By mistake, the vessel was navigated into the English Channel, was wrecked upon
the rugged coast of Wales, and went to pieces. Kieft, with eighty other persons, including Bogardus and the Fiscal, were lost; only twenty were saved.
Melyn, the *patroon* of Staten Island, floated on his back, landed on a sand-
bank, and thence reached the mainland in safety. Kuyter, founder of new
Harlem was also saved.

On the 11th of May, 1647, Governor Stuyvesant, as "redresser-general" of
all the colonial abuses, arrived at Manhattan to enter upon an administration
which was to last until the end of the Dutch power over New Netherland.

Stuyvesant also, seems to have been the first governor who took pride in
the town itself. He found the infant city very unattractive—fences straggling,
cattle running around loose, the public ways crooked, many of them encroach-
ing on the lines of the street, and half the houses in a tumble-down condition.
All these evils he at once set about to remedy; and one of his earliest acts was
to appoint the first "Surveyors of Buildings," whose duties were to regulate
the erection of new houses in New Amsterdam.

The Dutch Company " now resolved to open to private persons the trade,
which it had exclusively carried on with New Netherland, the Virginia, the
Swedish, English, and French colonies, or other places thereabout," and the
new Director and Council were ordered to be vigilant in enforcing all colonial
custom-house regulations. All cargoes to New Netherland were to be exam-
ined, on arrival, but the custom-house officers, and all who were homeward
bound were to give bonds for the payment of duties in Holland. Nor was it
long before Stuyvesant had an opportunity of showing his zeal.

About this period, 1648, it became necessary to regulate the taverns, as
almost one-fourth of the town of New Amsterdam had become houses for the

sale of brandy, tobacco, or beer. No new taverns, it was ordained, should be licensed, except by unanimous consent of the Director and his Council; and those established might continue four years longer, if their owners would abstain from selling to the savages, report all brawls and occupy decent houses, "to adorn the town of New Amsterdam." Notwithstanding, however, all these precautions, the Indians were daily seen "running drunk through the Manhattans." New York, now the metropolitan city, witnesses every day and night crowds of such drunken savages in her streets; and it would almost seem that our wise legislators have not wisdom or strength enough to frame laws to subdue or prevent this public evil of all evils. At last, at New Amsterdam, in addition to the former penalties, offenders against the temperance laws were now " to be arbitrarily punished, without any dissimulation."

In the year 1648, no person was allowed to carry on business, except he was a permanent resident, and had taken the oath of allegiance, was worth from two thousand to three thousand guilders, at least, and intended to keep " fire and light in the province." This was an early expression of permanent residence in the Dutch province. Old residents, however, not possessing the full trade qualifications, were allowed the same privilege, provided they remained only in the province and used only the weights and measures of " Old Amsterdam," and, " to which we owe our name." Scotch merchants and pedlers were not forgotten in these arrangements, for it was also ordained, that " all Scotch merchants and dealers, who come over from their own country with the intention of trading here," should "not be permitted to carry on any trade in the land " until they had resided here three years. They were also required to build a " decent, habitable tenement," one year after their arrival. Every Monday was to be market-day, and, in imitation of *fatherland*, an annual " keemis," or fair, for ten days, was established, commencing on Monday after St. Bartholomew's Day, at which all persons could sell goods from their tents.

At last, a naval war, long brewing, broke out between England and the United Provinces, and, without warning, Dutch ships were arrested in English ports, and the crews impressed. Martin Harpertsen Tromp commanded the Dutch fleet. His name has no prefix of " Van," as many writers insist. Bancroft and Broadhead are among the few who have not adopted the common error. The Dutch Admiral was no more " Van Tromp " than the English was "Van Blake," or our brave American "Van Farragut." Tromp, in a few days, met the British fleet, under Admiral Blake, in Dover Straits, and a bloody but indecisive fight followed. Brilliant naval engagements ensued, in which Tromp and De Ruyter, with Blake and Ayscue, immortalized themselves. But the first year of hostilities closing with a victory, Blake sought refuge in the Thames, when the Dutch commander placed a broom at the masthead, an emblem or token that he had swept the British Channel free from British ships. These hostilities between Holland and England encouraged pirates and robbers to infest the shores of the East River, and perpetrate excesses on Long Island and the neighborhood of New Amsterdam. Several yachts were immediately commissioned to act against the pirates. A reward of one hundred thalers was offered for each of the outlaws, and a proclamation issued prohibiting all persons from harboring them, under the penalty of banishment and the confiscation of their goods. Forces had even been collected to act against New Netherland, but the joyful intelligence of peace sent them to dislodge the French from the coast of Maine; and thus, for ten years longer, the coveted Dutch-American province continued under the sway of Holland. The peace was published "in the ringing of bell from City Hall," on the 12th of August, 1654, appointed, piously, by Stuyvesant, as a day of general thanksgiving.

During the same month, 1654, Le Moyne, a Jesuit father and missionary to the Indians, immortalized his name by a discovery which afterward formed one of the largest sources of wealth in our State. Reaching the entrance of a small lake filled with salmon-trout and other fish, he tasted the water of a spring which his Indian guides were afraid to drink, saying that there was a demon in them which rendered it offensive. But the Jesuit had discovered a "fountain of salt water," from which he actually made salt as natural as that of the sea. Taking a sample, he descended the Onedia, passed over the Ontario and the St. Lawrence, and safely reached Quebec with the intelligence of his wonderful discovery. To the State of New York it has since been more valuable than a mine of silver or gold ; located at Syracuse.

During the year of 1654, the Swedish and the Casimir colonists on the Delaware had taken the Dutch fort there; soon after, Stuyvesant had an opportunity of retaking the *Golden Stork*, a Swedish ship, bound to South River, which, by mistake entered Sandy Hook, and anchored behind Staten Island. His error discovered, the Captain sent a boat to Manhattan for a pilot, when the Governor ordered the crew to the guard-house, and dispatched soldiers to seize the vessel. The *Spark's* cargo was removed to the Company's magazine until a reciprocal restitution should have been made. The Swedish agent sent a long protest to Governor Stuyvesant, complaining of his conduct.

In the year 1656, there were in New Amsterdam, one hundred and twenty houses and one thousand souls. A proclamation now forbid the removal of any crops in the town or colony, until the Company's tithes had been paid. The authorities of Rensselaerswyck refusing to publish this notice, the tapsters were sent down to New Amsterdam, pleading that they acted under the orders of their feudal officers. This defence was overruled, and one fined two hundred pounds, and another eight hundred guilders.

In the year 1657, " in conformity to the custom of the City of Amsterdam in Europe," this great burgher right was introduced into New Amsterdam. This was an absurd imitation of an invidious policy, and the mother city herself was soon obliged to abandon it; notwithstanding Governor Stuyvesant attempted to establish, in New Amsterdam this most offensive of all distinctions—an aristocracy founded on a class or mere wealth.

During the year 1659, it was discovered that the Dutch colony had as yet produced no returns, and was already seven thousand guilders in arrears. It was therefore determined that, to prevent further loss, such colonists only as had left Holland before December, 1658, should be provided with provisions. Goods were to be sold only for cash, and exemptions from tithes and taxes were to cease over several years before the stipulated period, and merchandise thereafter was to be consigned to the City of Amsterdam exclusively. The colonists remonstrated against this new restriction of trade, which had the appearance of gross slavery and of fostering the free prospects of a worthy people. This remonstrance was well-timed, and the City Council consented that all the traders on the South River might export all goods, except peltry, to any place they wished.

In the year 1660, a second survey and map of New Amsterdam was made by Jacques Cortelyon, and the city was found to contain three hundred and fifty houses. It was sent to the Amsterdam Chamber, in case it should be thought " good to make it more public by having it engraved." The restoration of Charles the Second, in 1661, did not produce in England more friendly feelings towards the Dutch ; and the two nations now became commercial rivals. The Act of Navigation had already closed the ports of New England, Virginia and Maryland, against Holland and its Colony of New Netherland. Such, at that time was the narrow spirit of British statesmen, and many Independents and Dissenters desired to seek new homes, where they would be alike free from monarchy, prelacy, and British rule.

A number of breweries, brick-kilns, and other manufactories, carried on a successful business; and the potteries on Long Island, some persons esteemed equal to those of Delft. Dirck De Wolf having obtained from the Amsterdam Chamber, in 1661, the exclusive privilege of making salt for seven years in New Netherland, began its manufacture upon Coney Island; but the Gravesend settlers, who claimed the spot, arrested the enterprise; and this, too, notwithstanding Governor Stuyvesant sent a military guard to protect him.

In the year 1664, the population of New Netherland had increased to "full ten thousand," and New Amsterdam contained one thousand five hundred, and wore an appearance of great prosperity. English jealousy evidently increased with the augmenting commerce of the Dutch. James, Duke of York, was the King's brother, and also the Governor of the African Company, and he denounced the Dutch West India Company, which had endeavored to secure the territory on the Gold Coast from English speculators and intruders. England resolved to march a step further, and, at one blow, to rob Holland of her American province. The King granted a sealed patent to the Duke of York for a large territory in America, including Long Island and all the lands and rivers from the west side of the Connecticut to the east side of the Delaware Bay. This sweeping grant embraced the whole of New Netherland.

The Duke of York, that he might lose no time in securing his patent, dispatched Captain Scott, with one hundred and fifty followers, to visit the Island of Manhattan, the value of which was now estimated at three thousand pounds. On the 11th of January, 1664, the valarous Scott made his appearance at "Brenelen" Ferry Landing, and, with great flourish of trumpets, demanded submission to the English flag. Governor Stuyvesant, dispatching his Secretary, politely asked Captain Scott, "Will you come across the river?" and the reply was, "No; let Stuyvesant come over with one hundred soldiers; I will wait for him here." "What for?" demanded the Secretary. "I would run him through the body," was the Captain's courteous answer. "That would not be a friendly act," replied the Governor's deputy. Thus they parted. Scott retiring to Midwout (Flatbush), with his forces, with drums beating and colors flying, while the people "locked on with wonder, not knowing what it meant. Scott told them they must abandon their allegiance to the Dutch, and promised to confer with Governor Stuyvesant. But when he reached the river, on his way to New Amsterdam, for this purpose, he declined crossing it. Still, he felt very brave, *threatening* to go over, proclaim the English King at the Manhattans, and "rip the guts" and cut the feet from any man who says, "This is not the King's land." This was, certainly very bloodthirsty; but the good people of Manhattan all escaped with whole feet and bowels. The valiant Captain then marched into New Utrecht; ordered the only gun of which the block-house boasted to be fired in the King's honor, and continued his triumphant march to Amersfort, for another bloodless victory.

Governor Stuyvesant now ordered a new commission to confer with Captain Scott, at Jamaica, and Cornelis Steenwyck—one of the fathers of New Amsterdam, residing on his farm at Harlem—was one of the commission. It was here agreed that the English captain should hereafter desist from disturbing the Dutch towns. The latter, however, insisted that the basis of future negotiations, should recognize Long Island as belonging to Great Brittain. He also hinted that the Duke of York intended to reduce, in time, the whole province of New Netherland—a declaration which was to prove true sooner than the Dutch Governor anticipated.

In September of the same year (1664), Colonel Nicholls anchored before New Amsterdam with a fleet and soldiers. His imperious message to Governor Stuyvesant was: "I shall come with ships and soldiers raise the white flag of peace at the fort, and then something may be considered." The Dutch colony was entirely unprepared for such a warlike visit, and capitulated at eight o'clock on the morning of September 8th, 1664. Stuyvesant, at the head of the garrison, marched out of the fort with the honors of war, pursuant to the terms of the surrender. His soldiers were immediately led down the "*Bever's Paatje*," on Beaver Lane, to the shore of the North River, where they embarked for Holland. An English "corporal's guide" immediately entered and took possession of the fort, over which the English flag was at once hoisted. Its name, Fort Amsterdam, was then changed to "Fort James," and New Amsterdam was henceforth known as "New York." This was a violent and treacherous seizure of territory at a time of profound peace—a breach of private justice and public faith; and by it, a great state had imposed on it a name which is unknown in history, save as it is connected with bigotry and tyranny, and which has ever been an enemy of political and religious liberty.

Before following farther the course of events, a rapid retrospect of the commercial prosperity of New Netherland seems desirable. At the period when Governor Stuyvesant's administration was so suddenly terminated by the Duke of York's forces, the population of New Netherland was established at "full ten thousand." When New Amsterdam was first surveyed, in 1656, it contained one hundred and twenty houses, and one thousand souls, which increased to fifteen hundred in 1664.

Although *wampum* or "*zawan*" had become almost the exclusive currency of New Netherlands (1664), still, beaver remained the standard of value. During the years 1651-2, Director Stuyvesant tried to introduce a specie currency, and applied to Holland for twenty-five thousand guilders in Dutch shillings and four-penny pieces, but the Directors there disapproved of his project. The people were thus entirely dependent on *wampum*, as we are upon "greenbacks," and the value of wages, property, and every commodity, was, in consequence, seriously disturbed. So it is in this day, and ever will be, with an irredeemable currency, whether of clam shells, thin paper or anything else, not equal to specie. At first *wampum* passed at the rate of four black beads for one stiver; next it was lowered to six, and in 1657 to eight, and then ordered to be considered a tender for gold and silver. To a similar level our wiseacre financiers would now reduce our paper-money. But Stuyvesant wisely objected, as it would bring the value of property to naught. In the year 1659, the white *wampum* was next reduced from twelve to sixteen, and the black from six to eight for a stiver. What was the result? The holder was obliged to give more *wampum* for any article he purchased from the trader, who, in return, allowed the natives a large quantity of it for his beavers and skins; and, to use the plain record of the day, "little or no benefit accrued." Nominally, prices advanced when beavers which had sold for twelve and fourteen (guilders) rose to twenty-two and twenty-four, bread from fourteen to twenty-two stivers—eight-pound loafs—loaf nine to ten stivers per pound, pork fifteen to twenty stivers, shoes from three and a half guilders to twelve a pair, and wrought iron from eighteen to twenty stivers the pound. Beavers and specie remained all the while of equal value; but the difference between these and *wampum* was fifty per cent. The effect on wages was almost ruinous. An old record says: "The poor farmer, laborer, and public officer, being paid in *wampum*, are almost reduced to the necessity of living on alms."

The war which broke out in 1672 between the English and the Dutch, and which was chiefly carried on by the natives of the two powers, occasioned apprehensions for the safety of the Province of New York; and Governor Lovelace, the successor of Nicholls, the first English Governor, made preparations for a demonstration of that character on the part of the Dutch. Nor were his fears unfounded; although some months elapsing without any appearance of the enemy, he allowed himself to fall into a fatal sense of security, and accordingly disbanded the levies, while he himself departed on a visit to the Eastern colonies, leaving the fort in charge of Captain John Manning. The Dutch, however, were not asleep; nor had they relinquished their design. Determined to regain New Amsterdam at all hazards, they fitted out a fleet of five ships, commanded by Admirals Benckes and Evertsen, with Captains Colve, Boes, and Van Zye. On the 30th of July, 1673, they appeared off Sandy Hook; and quietly sailing up the bay, and anchoring before Staten Island, soon appeared opposite the Battery. The fleet then opened a heavy cannonade upon the city, at the same time that Captain Colve, landing with six hundred men, drew up in order of battle on the Commons, ready to march into the city. At a given signal, the men marched down Broadway, whereupon Captain Manning surrendered the fort, on condition that its garrison should march out with all the honors of war. This condition having been granted, the Dutch troops again possessed the fort and city. New York received the name of New Orange, and the fort itself the name of Fort William Hendrick. Governor Lovelace, who, meanwhile, had hastened back from his pleasure tour, was allowed to return with the Dutch Admiral only; however, to receive from the English Government a severe reprimand for cowardice and treachery, and to learn that his estates had been confiscated to the Duke of York.

Captain Colve, now in command of the Province of New Netherland, received a commission from Benckes and Evertsen to govern the new territory. His rule, though brief, was energetic. He at once took measures to improve the defenses of the fort; and in October, 1673, we find it stated in one of his orders that the fortifications had then, at great expense and labor to the citizens and inhabitants, been brought "to perfection." Anthony De Milt was appointed Schout, with three burgomasters and five schepens. The entire city assumed the appearance of a military post, the Commons (the present park) becoming the parade-ground. A walk or palisade was placed around it, running from Trinity Church along Wall street--hence its name—and blockhouses protected the settlement on every side. Every day the Schout reviewed the military, before the "Stadt Huys," at the head of Coenties Slip. At six in the evening he received the city keys, and with a guard of six men locked the public gates, and stationed the sentinels. He unlocked the gates at sunrise. The city at this period numbered three hundred and twenty-two houses.

But the second administration of the Dutch was destined to be of short duration. On the 9th of February, 1674, the treaty of peace between England and the States-General was signed at Westminster; and the Dutch, having discovered and possessed the beautiful country of New Netherlands for almost sixty years, were now, once and forever, dispossessed of it. On that day the old fort again became "Fort James," having surrendered to Sir Edmund Andrews, who had been appointed Governor by the Duke of York.

The Dutch of New Amsterdam were distinguished for their good nature, love of home, and cordial hospitality. Fast young men, late hours, and fashionable dissipation were unknown. There was, nevertheless, plenty of opportunity for healthful recreation. Holidays were abundant, each family having some of its own, such as birthdays, christenings, and marriage anniversaries. Each season, too, introduced its own peculiar and social festivals—the "Quilting," "Apple-Raising," and "Husking Bees." The work on such occasions was soon finished, after which the guests sat down to a supper, well supplied with chocolate and waffles—the evening terminating with a merry dance. Dancing was a favorite amusement. The slaves danced to the music of their rude instruments, in the markets; while the maidens and youths practised the same amusement at their social parties, and around the annual May-Pole, on the "Bowling Green."

Besides such holidays five public or national festivals were observed. These were: *Kersteydt*, or Christmas; *Nieuw Jar*, or New Year; *Paas*, or Passover; *Pinkster*, Whitsuntide; and *Santa Claus*, St. Nicholas, or Chris-Kinkle Day. The morn of the Nativity was hailed with universal salutations of a "Merry Christmas"—a good old Knickerbocker custom which has descended unimpaired to us. Next, in the day's programme, came "Turkey Shooting"—the young men repairing either to the "Beekman Swamp," or on the Common (Park), for this amusement. Each man paid a few stivers for a "chance," when the best shot obtained the prize. The day was also commemorated, as it is at the present day, by family dinners, and closed with domestic gayety and cheerfulness.

New-Year's Day was devoted to the universal interchange of visits. Every door in New Amsterdam was thrown wide open, and a warm welcome extended to the stranger as well as the friend.

Santa Claus, however, was *the* day of all others with the little Dutch folk, for it was sacred to St. Nicholas—the tutelar divinity of New Amsterdam, who had presided at the figure-head of the first emigrant ship that reached her shores. The first church erected within her fort was also named after St. Nicholas. He was, to the imagination of the little people, a jolly, rosy-cheeked, little old man, with a slouched hat, large Flemish nose, and a very long pipe. His sleigh, loaded with all sorts of Christmas gifts, was drawn by reindeer; and, as he drove rapidly over the roofs of the houses, he would pause at the chimneys to leave presents in the stockings of the good children: if *bad*, they might expect nothing but a switch or leather-strap. In this way the young Knickerbockers became models of good behavior and propriety.

About 1750, the *sconce* came in fashion—a hanging or projecting candle-stick, with a mirror to reflect the rays. This was a very showy article, giving a fine light to the rooms. After this period, pier and mantle glasses came into fashion. Pictures, such as they were, abounded; but they were for the most part poor engravings of Dutch cities and naval engagements. Chintz calico of inferior quality formed the only window curtains, without any cornices. There were no carpets among the early Dutch, nor any in general use among New Yorkers until up to the period of the Revolution. The famous Captain Kidd, it is said, owned the first modern carpet in his best room, and the pirate's house was the best furnished in the city. It was made of Turkey work, at a cost of twenty-five dollars, and resembled a large rug. The custom of sanding the floor of the principal room, or parlor, was universal, and much taste was displayed in the many fanciful devices and figures made in the sand with the brooms of the smart Dutch matrons and daughters. Our Holland ancestors knew nothing of lounges or sofas, or even that comfortable American invention, the rocking-chair. Their best chairs were straight and high-backed, covered with Russia leather, and elaborately ornamented with double and triple rows of brass nails. In addition to these, the parlor was decorated with one or two chairs having embroidered seats and backs, the handiwork of the daughters. Some of the oldest families also displayed in their best rooms two chairs with cushions of tapestry, or velvet, trimmed with lace. About the year 1700, cane seats became fashionable, and thirty years after came the leather chairs, worth from five to ten dollars each. These led the fashion about thirty years more, when mahogany and black walnut chairs, with their crimson damask cushions, appeared.

But the most ornamental piece of furniture in the parlor was the bed, with its heavy curtains and valance of camlet. No mattresses then, but a substantial bed of live geese feathers, with a very light one of down for the covering. These beds were the boast and pride of the most respectable Dutch matrons, and, with their well-filled chests of home-made linen, supplied their claims to skill in housekeeping. A check covering cased the beds and pillows; the sheets were made of homespun linen, and over the whole was thrown a bedquilt of patchwork, wrought into every conceivable shape and pattern.

The horses in these days were bred wild in the woods and pastures which covered the upper part of Manhattan Island. Thousands of them ran at large —the owners, at certain seasons, branding them with their names, when they turned them loose again, until winter rendered a shelter for them necessary. Such was their great increase, that it is said the Island was overrun by the animals, now become as wild and dangerous as the buffaloes of the praries; the breed was, consequently, inferior, the price of a horse ranging from ten dollars to forty dollars, according to the strength, and not the speed of the animal.

The literature of New Amsterdam was entirely different from that of modern times. In the place of the novels, magazines and light reading which now fill the center-tables, there was to be found little else than Bibles, Testaments and psalm-books. The matrons' church books were generally costly bound, with silver clasps and edgings, and sometimes of gold. These were suspended to the girdle by silver and gold chains, and distinguished the style of the families using them, on the Sabbath days.

The Sundays in New Amsterdam were, moreover, better observed by its inhabitants than at the present day. All classes arrayed in their best, then attended the public services of religion: and the people, almost exclusively Calvinists, attended the Dutch Reformed Church.

At funerals, it was the custom to give hot wine in water, and wine-sangaree in summer. Ladies generally attended on such mournful occasions, especially if the deceased was a female, when burnt wine was served in silver tankards. At a later era, on the death of Mrs. Daniel Phoenix, the wife of the City Treasurer, all the pall-bearers were ladies.

The working-man always wore his leather apron, no matter what his employment. Tradesmen were accustomed to saw his own wood; and a most healthful exercise it was. Nor did any man in middle circumstances fear to carry home his "one hundred weight" of meal from market. On the contrary, it would have been considered a disgrace to have avoided such a burden.

Sleighing was a fashionable amusement: and a ride to Harlem became the longest drive among the "city folk." Parties, however, often turned aside to visit "Hell Gate," influenced, doubtless, by the fact that on this road, over the Tankill (a little stream emptying into the Harlem River, opposite Blackwells' Island), was the "*Kissing Bridge*," so laid down on the maps, and named from the old Dutch custom of the gentlemen saluting their lady companions whenever they crossed the bridge.

To sum up, the earliest Dutch emigrants to New York left their deep impress upon the city and upon the State. Far-reaching commerce, which immortalized Old Amsterdam in the seventeenth century, soon provoked the envy of New Amsterdam's neighbors, and in the end made our city the emporium of the Western World. Our ancestors left children and children's children, who were well fitted to act important parts in the great work of opening the American continent to European and Christian civilization. They brought with them honest maxims, industry, and the liberal ideas of their *Fatherland* —their schoolmasters, their dominies, and their BIBLES. In the course of events, however, New Netherland passed over to British rule, when new customs, new relationships, and new habits of thought, were introduced.

SMALL TALK

Steam Job, Book, Newspaper

AND COMMERCIAL

Printing Establishment!

225 and 227 East 129th St.

First class printing in all its branches at rates comparing favorably with any in New York.

The smallest Label or the largest Poster furnished at Short notice.

Association, Lodge and Church Printing a Specialty.

Estimates Cheerfully Furnished.

Orders by mail promptly attended to and canvassers with samples sent to any address.

HARLEM BUSINESS DIRECTORY.

Architect.
Charles Dexter, 2260 Third Avenue.

Bakers.
Ardrew Wilbam, 2071 Third Avenue.
M. A. Beyer, 2452 Fourth Avenue.

Barbers.
Adam Dietrich, 155 East 125th Street.
Henry Fried, 2349 Third Avenue.

Beer Saloons.
Emil Hoss, 2193 Third Avenue.

Billiards.
Henry Wagner, 2517 Third Avenue.

Boats to Let.
O. P. Raynor, Harlem Bridge.

Bookbinders.
Perkinson & Lennon, 225 East 119th Street.

Boots & Shoes.
J. Goodman, 2216 Third Avenue.
J. Krieks, 2182 Third Avenue.
W. E. Rice & Co., 2289 Third Avenue.
F. Whitehouse, 2116 Third Avenue.
N. Zabinski, 2253 Third Avenue.
H. Zabinski, 2220 Third Avenue.

Burglar Alarms.
Jos. I. Conklin & Co., Lexington Avenue and 125th Street.

Builders' Hardware.
Thos. Farrell, 2489 Third Avenue.

Butter and Cheese.
Z. S. Rodgers, 2391 Third Avenue.

Carpenters & Builders.
L. Sullivan, 69 East 120th Street.
Thos. Dunwoody, 3d. Av., bet. 124th & 125th sts.
C. W. H. Eding, 2315 Fourth Avenue.

Carpets.
Croft Brothers, 2159 and 2161 Third Avenue.

Clock Maker.
L. J. Boucel, 171 East 125th street.

Clothiers.
Harlem & Westchester Clothing Co. 3d. Ave. cnd. 125th Street.
Stone & Goodman 2161 Third Avenue.

Coal & Wood.
W. A. White, 152 East 125th Street.

Cooked Meats & Provisions.
C. F. Rune, 2432 Third Avenue.

Dentists.
S. Cleland, 151 East 125th street
L. S. King, 2478 Third Avenue.
L. B. Lockwood, 70 East 127th Street

Druggists.
Clinton Hurd, 2461 Third Avenue,
M. A. Jackson, 2133 Third Avenue,
ad J. Nolan, 2 3 Third Avenue.
Axner & Ingerd, 162 West 125th.
Paul Weber, 2190 Third Avenue.
H. G. Weyh, 2152 Third Avenue.

Dry Goods.
F. Callan, Third Ave. & 121st Street.
Schildwachter & Becker, 2191 Third Avenue.

Dyers & Cleaners.
H. C. Bollman, 2431 Fourth avenue.
A. L. Soris, 2445 Third Avenue.

Electrical Apparatus.
Jos. I. Conklin & Co., Lexington Avenue and 125th Street.

Express.
Harlem Express Co., 205 East 125th Street.

Fancy Goods and Notions.
John Horne, 2473 Third Avenue.

Fish.
Robert Brown, 2205½ Third Avenue.

Flour & Feed.
C. D. Tooker, 280 Third Avenue.

Frames.
W. F. Thompson, 2318 Fourth Avenue.

Fruits.
Cullen & Mathews, 2 64 Third Avenue.

Furniture.
M. Antony, 2257 Third Avenue.
Geo. B. Terwell & Co., 2359 Third Ave.
Harlem & New York Furniture Co., 2183 & 2185 Third Avenue.

Gent's Furnishing Goods.
E. F. Hartley, 2336 Third Avenue
Charles King, 228 West 125th street.
Philip Sor, 423 Third Avenue.
I. Strauss, 2303 Third Avenue,

Goodyear Rubber Goods.
Headquarters 2197 Third Avenue.

Grinding.
Henry Picator, 226 East 125th Street.

Grocers.
James Ayers, 2365 Third Avenue.
M. L. Bamman & Co., Fourth Avenue and 2nd 125th Street.
Bennett & Jarvis, 2784 and 2351 Third Avenue.
Fletcher Bros. Third Avenue and 125th Street.
Wm. Robinson, 2416 Fourth Avenue.
S. C. Weber, 2455 Third Avenue.

Hardware and House Furnishing Goods.
Elford Dickerman, 2___ Third Avenue.

HARLEM BUSINESS DIRECTORY.

Hats.
I. Goldsmid, 2312 Third Avenue.
R. T. Kelly, 2327 Third Avenue.
(Manufacturer and Dealer.)

Hotels.
Daly's Hotel, 129th Street & Third Avenue
Everett Levi & Co. 2491 Third Avenue.
Mt. Morris Hotel, 125th St. & Mt. Morris Ave.
William Schwab, 2387 Third Avenue.
Warnken's Hotel, 12th St. & Ft. Nicholas Ave.

Ice Cream.
W. J. Sutherland, 2205 Third Avenue.

Intelligence Office.
Mrs. Mills, 227 West 125th Street

Industrial Insurance.
J. A. Megargee, 2281 Third Avenue.

Lawyers.
Felix Jellenik, 2245 Third Avenue.
Jos. H. McCarthy, Lexington Av. & 125th St.
W. K. Spencer, 436 East 117th Street.
Thos. H. Vickery, 2262 Third Avenue.

Livery Stables.
Robert Prior, 302, 4 & 6 East 120th Street.
125th Street and Grand Boulevard, and opposite Mott Haven Landing.

Lumber.
W. H. Colwell & Son, Third Av. & 128th St.

Machinists.
Roth & Briggs, 224 East 124th Street.

Masquerade Costumes.
J. Franklin, 2174 Third Avenue.

Meats.
M. Wilhelm, 2320 Third Avenue.

Millinery & Fancy Goods.
S. Hoffman, 2311 Third Avenue.
A. Piser, 2245 & 2247 Third Avenue.
D. M. Williams & Co., 2308 Third Avenue.

Millinery & Hair Goods.
Misses Hawkins, 2336 Third Avenue.

Music.
G. Speck & Son, 2240 Third Avenue.

Paints.
Haley, Doubleday & Co., 2146 Third Avenue.

Photographic Art Rooms.
E. P. Bulkeley, 2252 to 2258 Third Avenue.
W. L. Entsor Sko, 2308 Third Avenue.
James Ouick, Third Ave. & 125th Street.

Piano Forte Manufacturers.
Behning & Son, 129 East 125th Street.
Diehl & Zench, 2374 Third Avenue
Mathushek & Kingsbey, 210 East 125th Street.
Whitney & Co., 2374 Third Avenue.

Physicians.
D. Franklin, M. D., 153 East 117th Street.
Theo. D. C. Miller, 2008 Lexington Avenue.
Z. L. Leonard, 430 East 117th Street.

Plumbers.
Geo. B. Brown, 125th St. & Fourth Ave.
Daily & Fahridy, 2135 Third Avenue
Meany Bros., 188 East 124th Street.
Wm. Rosenwald, 2421 Fourth Avenue.

Printers.
Perkinson & Johnson, 235 East 129th Street.

Provision Dealers.
G. F. Keller & Sons, 2171 Third Avenue.

Ranges & Furnaces.
Graham & Murphy, 2621 Fourth Avenue.

Real Estate.
W. A. Armstrong, 2281 Third Avenue.
M. Barnett, S. E. cor. Fourth Ave. & 125th St.
Benjamin Browne 146 East 125th Street.
W. H. Folsom, 1454 Third Avenue.
R. A. Mills, 227 West 125th Street.
Rose & Crawford, Lexington Ave. & 125th St.
E. A. Reed, 162 East 125th Street.
Geo. H. Weyer, 2292 Third Avenue.

Restaurant.
James L. Sullivan, 2323 Third Avenue.
A. Taylor, 64 East 125th Street.

Segars and Tobacco.
John A. Baymayer 2730 Third Avenue.
Jacob Hagmayer, 2150 Third Avenue.
Owl Cigar Store, 2359 Third Avenue.
J. H. Rosen, & Co., 2364 Third Avenue.
Geo. W. Thompson, Third Avenue & 125th St.

Sewing Machines.
E. Raasch, 2151 Third Avenue.

Shooting Gallery.
James T. Kemp, 189 Third Avenue.

Sign Painters.
Vogut & Pooley, 162 East 125th Street.

Stationer.
George E. Gotthart, 2210 Third Avenue.
Wm. H. Entin, 2452 Third Avenue.
H. P. McGowan, jr., 142 East 125th Street.

Storage.
L. S. Dewey, 106 & 108 East 124th Street.

Undertakers.
Edward Gehlert, 2427 4th Avenue.
John W. Lyon, 74 East 125th Street.

Upholsterers.
L. Kruedelbach, 2622 Fourth Avenue.

Veterinary Surgeon.
Dr. M. L. Fry, 215 East 118th Street.

Wagon Builders.
Neukirk & Green, 144 East 129th Street.

Watches and Jewelry.
F. Keeping, 2147 Third Avenue.
F. C. Gleason, 2446 Third Avenue.

Wines and Delicatessen.
Lazarus & Stender, 2474 Third Avenue.
George Ruppel, 2261 Third Avenue.

Wines and Liquors.
George F. Cahill, Third Avenue.
French, 2575 Third Avenue.
R. Esterman, East 119th Street.
John Ryan, 2464 Third Avenue.

Wire Works.
J. Sullivan, 189 East 124th Street.

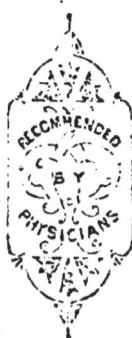

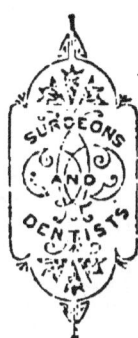

www.ingramcontent.com/pod-product-compliance
Lightning Source LLC
Chambersburg PA
CBHW022023080426
42733CB00007B/695